Home Away From Home

JOHN MARGOLIES

HOME
AWAY FROM HOME

· MOTELS · IN · AMERICA ·

A Bulfinch Press Book
Little, Brown and Company
Boston · New York · Toronto · London

CONTENTS

Chapter 1

Home Away From Home

The couple (top) who just arrived at the Underwood Motor Camp near Portland, Maine, would have cringed at the thought of having to traipse through the lobby of a luxurious hotel such as the Grand Salon of the Hotel Virginia in Long Beach, California.

It is 1900. Or 1905 or 1910. Tourists are getting behind the wheels of their tin lizzies and heading out into the hinterlands to see, experience, and discover their own United States in a whole new way. After decades of train travel, now they can choose their own routes and destinations on their own schedules. But going on an automobile trip at the turn of the century wasn't the casual adventure that it is today. In the early days, a vacation drive was more like an old-fashioned African safari or a polar expedition. Cars were expensive and unreliable contraptions. Roads were quagmires or booby traps. Moreover, facilities to serve this new breed of nomadic Americans just didn't exist.

So where did one stop along the way? There were all kinds of hostelries to serve the pre-automotive traveler. There were hotels, very often not so nice, located right by the tracks and the railroad station. There were fleabag hotels and boardinghouses here and there for anyone who dared to enter them. And then there were the luxury hotels —fancy, stuffy, and expensive—to serve the wealthy and cultivated clientele. These upper-crust accommodations contained not only rooms to sleep in, which were only part of their function and source of profit, but also elaborate public spaces—grand lobbies full of overstuffed furniture, marble staircases, formal dining rooms—and employees dressed to the nines in fancy uniforms.

But these old, established places to rest were not intended to serve travelers by automobile, although some used them. And many members of the motoring public didn't want to stay in hotels even if they could. In addition to being expensive, hotels separated the travelers from their cars. Motorists were often dressed in special clothing to withstand the rigors and hazards of automotive travel. Often the tourists would be covered with soot and grime, and the very thought of traipsing through fancy lobbies was an embarrassing idea at best. And what if the automobile traveler got caught out in the middle of nowhere as twilight was setting in, unable to make it to the next town?

The needs of these newfangled tourists demanded an array of lodging alternatives, and the American free-enterprise system and ingenuity resulted in new solutions. The

history of lodging in the twentieth century is a nonsequential and nearly simultaneous development of convenient and functional ways for people to get some sleep and then keep going: camping in free and rental spaces; tourist cabins (some free municipal ones, but most for rent); tourist homes where people would rent out spare bedrooms in their houses; combination camps, cabins, and tourist homes; motor courts, which became motels of low-slung continuous buildings full of bedrooms; and eventually, motor inns or motor hotels, which ended up providing many of the services and amenities of old downtown hotels, but with a more informal atmosphere in roadside settings.

Housing for motorists met the competi-

tion of hotels head-on. Camps, cabins, and motels offered many advantages. They were usually located on the outskirts of a town, saving the exhausted motorist the time and hassle of struggling with downtown traffic. Motorists could park their car immediately adjacent to the sleeping quarters, saving the time and bother of having to unload everything, and the expense of tipping a bellhop and paying for a parking place in a garage. The facilities were nearly always less expensive than those offered at a hotel, although the accommodations themselves were usually much "rougher"; and the whole atmosphere was more casual. These new roadside facilities were a study in ease and convenience for the motorist—no elaborate registration and

A two-panel painting by John Steuart Curry, which was reproduced in Fortune *magazine in 1934, captured the energy and fellowship at an early cabin camp. At the lower right an actress on vacation is seen in her "yacht on wheels," knitting while listening to the radio.*

shades of plastic. Only the bedding and towels were of a natural material.... In the bathroom two water tumblers were sealed in cellophane sacks with the words: 'These glasses are sterilized for your protection.' Across the toilet seat a strip of paper bore the message: 'This seat has been sterilized with ultra-violet light for your protection.' Everyone was protecting me and it was horrible. I tore the glasses from their covers. I violated the toilet-seat with my foot...."

The American motel had arrived. A 1940 article in *Business Week,* "America Takes to the Motor Court," reported that the seduction of the tourist and the acceptance of these new roadside institutions was complete: "Actually, the auto court represents more than a different mode of accommodation. It stands for a new way of life in tourism — a way that combines convenience, inexpensiveness and informality in a formula that is definitely clicking."

checkout ritual. Pay your money in advance and then leave whenever in the morning.

The roadside hostelries that evolved were not only creative and efficient institutions, but they became part of the ethos of American mobility and popular culture. The setting of a motel room or a tourist cabin has provided memorable moments in movies and literature. John Steinbeck, in his grand tour

of the United States with his dog-confidant Charley, had some unforgettable encounters with the tourist lodging industry, including one night near Bangor, Maine: "...I stopped at an auto court and rented a room. It wasn't expensive. The sign said 'Greatly Reduced Winter Rates.' It was immaculate; everything was done in plastics — the floors, the curtain, table tops of stainless burnless plastic, lamp-

South of the Border, a motel and tourist attraction just south of the North Carolina border, uses humorous serial billboards to attract sleepy customers.

SIGNS

A mind-boggling sign can be a motel's greatest attribute. The sign is almost always the motorist's first encounter with a roadside hostelry and the nature of its facilities. These roadside beacons sometimes defy reason and logic in attracting their potential clientele — exhausted travelers in search of a regenerative, quiet spot to spend a night before continuing their journey. Motel owners choose catchy, evocative, and sometimes humorous nomenclature to distinguish themselves from their competitors. The signs shown on these pages depict such diverse subject matter as flora, fauna, modes of transportation, the owners' names, or the quality or type of the establishment. The prevailing rule is "anything goes," but if the message projected by the sign doesn't work, everyone goes...someplace else.

Shamrock, Texas

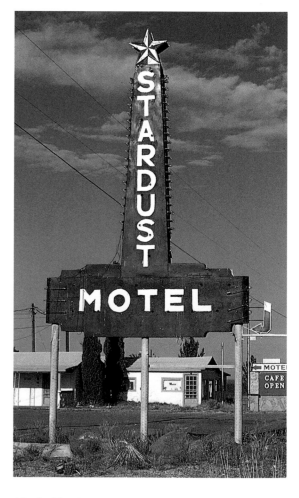

Marfa, Texas

St. Clair, Missouri

Salt Lake City, Utah

Durango, Colorado

Springfield, Missouri

Reno, Nevada

Burlington, Iowa

Burley, Idaho

Blair, Nebraska

Montgomery, Alabama

Lewiston, Maine

Joplin, Missouri

Austin, Texas

La Vale, Maryland

13

Chapter 2

Auto Camping

Long before the time of fully equipped motels and streamers across toilet seats promising the ultimate sanitary protection, many early motorists had to fight the elements as well as the real or imagined "germs." In fact, early automobile touring was looked at as a form of camping. By 1913 automobiles were well into mass production and there were some 1,194,000 motor cars registered and on the move. Americans took to the road in a joyous frenzy even though there were great hardships in early auto travel—bad roads, axle-deep mud, hand-operated windshield wipers, and even the very jolting and uncomfortable process of driving itself.

GAMES
YOU LIKE TO PLAY
for
HOME, TRAVEL
and CAMP
A
COMBINATION of
Jack Straws
Black Cat
Hop in the Tub
Tiddledy Winks
Johnnie on the Spot
Checkers
Parker Brothers Inc
SALEM, MASSACHUSETTS · NEW YORK · CHICAGO

Many of these "auto gypsies" hated the thought of expensive and pretentious downtown hotels and rhapsodized about communing with nature. At the end of a hard day, at least in those early days, camping spots were easy to find. Adventurers could plop down on a glen beside a stream, in a farmer's field, or in a schoolhouse yard. In the early teens a man named Frederic Van De Water celebrated a new freedom of self-navigation and the feeling of national brotherhood it brought: "Our flivver and our tent enabled us to visualize America....There is a powerful national value in motor camping. It is bringing people face to face, tin supper plate to tin supper plate, with a holiday atmosphere about their meeting." But as the number of campers increased, so too did the "no camping" signs.

To cope with the meandering throngs, municipalities began to construct camping grounds, especially in the western United States. These campgrounds were built to express civic pride and to attract tourists; this also allowed the cities to regulate them.

A man named Major Percival was active in New York City's tourist trade in the 1920s. Camp New York and Camp Arden Hall were proclaimed as New York's "Great OUTDOOR HOTELS" in the Bronx, just "30 minutes from Times Square."

16

Many cities in the West and Midwest built free campgrounds to attract tourists, including Wisconsin Dells, Wisconsin, as seen in this post-card view from the 1920s.

By 1920, with some 12 million cars on the road, some 300 cities provided free tourist parks. By 1922 there were 1,000 such facilities, and the number jumped to 2,000 by 1923. Some of the municipal campgrounds became quite elaborate while others were just fenced-off fields.

The city of Denver was a leader in the provision of wayfarers' resting places. An article in a 1922 issue of *American Motorist* romantically proclaimed that "conquering Americans — red blooded, appreciative and progressive — fill the roads to this mile high municipality to free camping grounds." And all of this bluster was more than just propaganda. Overland Park, "a beautiful shady spot" opened in 1920, was Denver's third free campground (the first dated from 1915). It was a $250,000 extravaganza on 160 acres along the South Platte River. In 1921, 39,854 people in 11,087 vehicles stayed at Overland Park, and these numbers increased to 50,000 people and 15,000 vehicles in 1922. Overland Park boasted a 26-room, three-story community clubhouse with the usual basics such as tables, benches, and restrooms, as well as reading rooms, a barber shop, a laundry, verandas filled with rocking chairs, and a dance hall where "500 couples could glide at one time."

Breathless rhetoric often accompanied the phenomenon of "autobumming," as

The Elysian Park campgrounds in Los Angeles opened in 1920 and were declared to be the "best equipped in California." In 1923 the receipts of the camp were $8,330 and the expenses were $6,010.46, netting the city a profit of $2,319.54.

17

LOVERS LAANE REST CAMP.   JAMESTOWN. N.D.
-Grass.-Shade- ModernEquipment - Police Protection.-
#1001   White Drug Photo.
Pat.

Sinclair Lewis referred to it. A pair of men sharing the last name of Long, specifically J. C. and John D., wrote an entire volume about motor camping in 1923, in which they stated, "In the United States a new and increasing way of satisfying this desire for recreation and adventure has swept over the country. Motor camping has become a leading national pastime…. The immense popularity of motor camping is easy to understand when one realizes that this pastime is romantic, healthful, educative, and at the same time economical." And economical it was. One

account from the 1920s tells of a party of three who traveled for 37 days and 4,500 miles for running expenses of $247.50.

A very important consideration was what to bring along on one's freewheeling safari. Long and Long, as well as authors of countless articles in popular magazines, published long and short lists of essentials and not-so-essentials, including at least 50 variations of camp beds, tents of every shape and size, special clothing, and cooking equipment from the fairly simple to the simply elaborate. And all of this stuff was folded up

The serenity and charm of this tableau at Lovers Laane stands in sharp contrast to its advertised promise of "police protection."

into containers that were strapped to the running boards and backs of cars or stored within vehicles. Even the campers' children were folded up, joked at least one source.

And for those who didn't care to fold everything up and pack it aboard, there were specialized touring vehicles, from the meek and humble to the plush and luxurious. These vehicles were the forerunners of the trailers, motor homes, and recreational vehicles of today. Some early explorers remodeled trucks and cars with special camping bodies. One Texan, it was reported,

Early touring by automobile was looked upon as "roughing it," and camping out was a logical extension of this notion. This charming domestic scene was captured in the verdant splendor of the Roosevelt National Forest in Colorado in the 1920s.

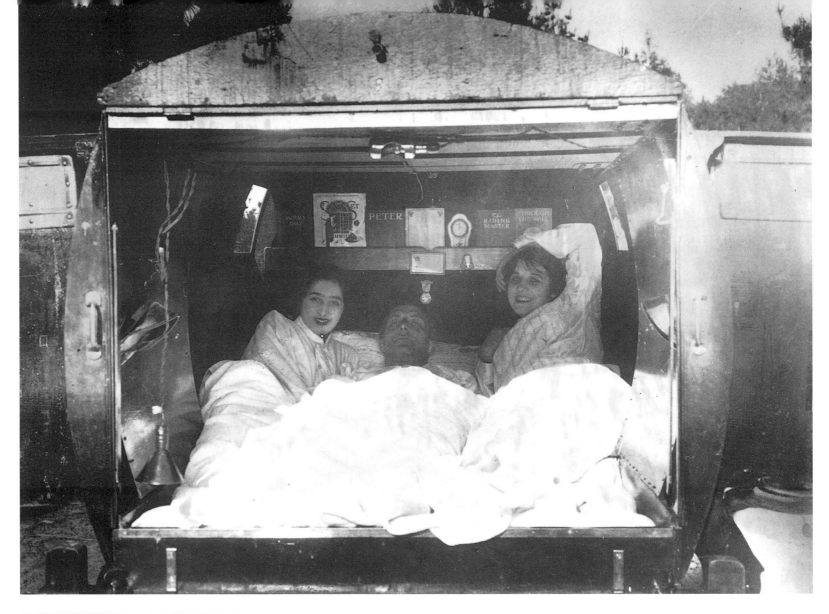

The Automobile Telescope Touring Apartment, perfected by a California inventor in 1916, was hailed as "one of the most interesting inventions ever made for the motor car." This deluxe home on wheels contained such amenities as hot water, clothes closets, dining table, and when its side was pulled outward, a bed where three could lie in comfort.

had a Cadillac 8 chassis with a $10,000 body, a "rolling home" with "a provision for every need, from writing desk and cook stove, to bath and toilet."

But the Automobile Telescope Touring Apartment invented and manufactured by Gustav de Bretteville in San Francisco in 1916 was even more complete and more luxurious than the Texan's Cadillac rig. The many-patented contraption was hailed in an

article in the *San Francisco Examiner* as "one of the most interesting inventions ever made for the motor car," one that was "more like a Pullman car than an automobile accessory." The Telescope, it was said, could be changed from car to complete camping outfit in less than two minutes. The side of the car pulled out so that the car interior became a bed. It had electric lights, shower, bath, and a seemingly dangerous heating device connected to the car's exhaust system.

At the other end of the spectrum we are told by Kenneth L. Roberts in his 1922 book, *Sun Hunters,* about a "hard-boiled bachelor" with a small Ford runabout who solved his breakfast problems on the road: "'In the morning', he explained, fondling his outfit with the proud and gentle hands of a parent, 'I get up and eat one of these individual packages of food. While I'm doing that the water is boiling for my coffee, and as soon as the coffee is done, I put on my frying pan with bacon and eggs in it. I use two paper napkins for my tablecloth. When I have finished breakfast, I put the eggshells in the breakfast-food box, wipe out the frying pan with the napkins, put them into the box

In this hand-tinted photograph, a lone automotive adventurer with a lot on his plate as well as on his running board, enjoys an informal repast on the road.

on top of the eggshells, and touch a match to the box. That cleans everything up.'"

The immense popularity of the municipal free campground ultimately led to the creation of private campgrounds and to the demise and disappearance of the original city camping grounds. James Agee, in a seminal article in *Fortune* in 1934, saw in the arrival of private campgrounds the beginning of the motel industry: "...Then some inspired misfit sewed the seed of a new profession by roping off his own backyard and introducing the

profit motive into automobile camping — space free, feed and services for gold. The automobile camp became a cash crop."

First farmers and others began to fence off fields and rake in the profits from the passing parade. Then oil companies and gas stations got into the act.

Beside a gas station five miles outside of Augusta, Georgia, as described in a 1929 article in *National Petroleum News,* the Peoples Oil Company offered a 1.5-acre pine grove for rent to campers. It also offered a

tea room, a stock of groceries, and a "log cabin establishment for toasted sandwiches." But the pièce de résistance was a small menagerie on the premises inhabited by a black bear, a monkey, an alligator, some peacocks, and some squirrels. The road was nearly blocked at times on Sunday afternoons to see the bear, which was trained to drink soda pop from bottles. "Often an automobile load of people will thus be tempted to drink with him," reported *NPN.* "The bear imbibes about 40 cold drinks a day and the proprietor

KOONTZ & WIFE
BEDFORD, PA.
NS CONTINENTAL
TOUR

of the place frequently sells as much as 15 cases of drink on Sunday."

By the late 1920s the glamour and rhetoric espousing camping were beginning to pale as the more sobering realities of the great pastime became more evident. Auto campers started to come under fire, although one positive account of the period describes them as "only gypsies for a few days, or weeks, as the case may be" but at other times "the most conventional of people." Other voices were harsher, describing the campers

as "tin-can tourists" because of the great assortment of canned goods they carried along, with "the insignia of their small order, a soup-can mounted on the radiator of the member's car." In Florida, "tin-canners" would spend the winter on the dole, sending their kids to school for 50 cents a week. Another critic stated that "these automobile hoboes are about as welcome in Florida as a rattlesnake at a strawberry festival." The same problem existed in California as well: "With their household goods piled

Mr. and Mrs. S. H. Koontz obviously traveled in style during their transcontinental tour circa 1925. The Koontzes were suitably attired for their meal in the wilderness in front of their house car in Bedford, Pennsylvania.

The tandem Streamlite was typical of trailers manufactured in the 1940s and 1950s, when such tow-along vehicles became longer, wider, and more elaborate.

high on the little car, their children tucked in unbelievably small places, and the dog riding joyously on the running-board, innumerable penniless invaders are swarming into the Golden State. Their capital, we are told, consists of "a dirty dollar bill and a dirty shirt, and they have no intention of changing either." At some of the more elaborate free municipal camps, time limits on the length of stay were imposed on the free spirits.

Many municipal camps were abolished as a nuisance because of the transients who stayed in them for protracted periods, begged from people in town, and "hung out unsightly wash." "Better class" people began to avoid them, it was reported. Local opposition came from those who thought that free campgrounds weren't a legitimate function of government and that they created sanitation problems. Hotel owners wanted them to disappear because they were looking

for paying customers. By the early 1930s the auto campers with all of their worldly possessions strapped to their cars, and the sometimes elaborate facilities that were built to accommodate them, were a not-so-fond memory.

But the auto camping experience lives on to this day. The campgrounds in our national and state parks are extremely popular as vacation destinations, and a spot in the woods in places like Yellowstone and Yosemite is nearly impossible to find in peak season. And the phenomenon of the trailer and the trailer park have spawned an entire subculture. Trailers have experienced a steady surge of popularity in the past 60 years. Major trailer companies vie with one another to create the spiffiest and niftiest creations, and sophisticated trailer parks, little and sometimes not-so-little, have evolved into cities catering to today's generation of "auto gypsies."

Happy campers pose in a Michigan state park in this real-photo postcard from the 1930s. Food and comfort were on the mind of the man who sent this postcard: "Fish biting fine. If you come bring pillow—onions, carrots."

Section view of Zagelmeyer camping trailer in open configuration, 1928.

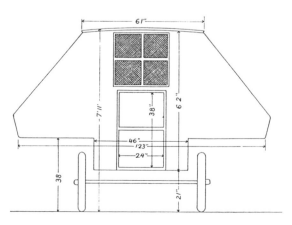

24

Although tourist cabins and motels had long before become the option of choice for most travelers, auto camping continued to enjoy great popularity as evidenced in this 1938 photograph of a congested campground in the San Bernardino National Forest in California.

Chapter 3

Cabins and Courts

The tourist cabin was a great idea for the less adventuresome and, yes, the lazier automobile traveler in the early part of this century. The thought of a preexisting roof over one's head was certainly an attractive alternative to camping out in the wild. The very first tourist court in the United States, at least according to *Ripley's Believe It or Not!* and other sources, was begun in 1901 in Douglas, Arizona, by a man named Tom Askins as housing for workers in nearby copper-smelting plants.

26

Delavan, Kansas.

The Delavan, Kansas, Camp House, opened in 1914, was built by the city, and its two apartments with inside garages were offered to motorists for no charge on a first-come, first-served basis.

In Askins Cottage Camp on the north side of town, there were nine cabins, T-shaped in plan with a bedroom, kitchenette, and a front room that could be used as a second bedroom, and each unit rented for 50 cents a night. With the advent of the automotive tourist trade the complex became Askins Tourist Court and then Askins Auto Court.

Like the early city-owned auto camps, the Delavan, Kansas, Camp House was proudly described as "the first municipal free hotel in the U.S." Opened in March 1914, it had two bedrooms and a garage for two cars within the same building. The rooms were equipped with beds, furniture,

A handcrafted biplane sign proffered inexpensive cabins and more at a camp near San Diego, California.

While tourist cabins and camps proliferated in the West and Midwest, tourist homes were a more common lodging alternative in East. The Colonial Manor was a typical example, offering Beautyrest beds along Main Street in Jacksonville, Florida.

A tire-like arch formed an inviting entryway to this auto camp along Highway 101 in King City, California.

Gas station–grocery stores often served as offices for tourist and auto camps in the 1920s and 1930s, seen here at "Camp Mc," location unknown.

cooking utensils, dishes, and cutlery. There was no key — the door was open to serve tourists on a first-come, first-served basis. And come they did. It was occupied nearly every night after it opened, and the town made plans to accommodate six cars and their occupants by 1916.

Most tourist cabins were located in the southern and western United States. In the Northeast and Midwest the growth was slower, with tourist homes filling the void. These establishments were usually a private house on a main thoroughfare with one or two rooms for rent and a sign out front announcing availability or lack thereof.

29

For a rental fee of 75 cents a tourist at Camp Grande in El Paso, Texas, could rent a space under Rustic Row, a long shed with pine logs and a roof of pine log slabs.

Camp Grande was built on 10 acres along the main highway in 1923. Its design, including an ornate entrance, was described as being in the "Indian Mission style of architecture."

All guests at Camp Grande, regardless of the nature of their sleeping quarters, were given access to shared communal facilities, including a recreation hall, 66 by 20 feet, with a dance floor and wide porches with hickory chairs.

Another lodging alternative at Camp Grande was a "bungalette," a tourist cabin by any other name. These units, renting for two dollars and up, were completely furnished and contained at least one bedroom, living room, kitchenette, and private bath.

Camp Grande in El Paso, Texas, was a hybrid between an auto camp and a cabin camp, and it combined some of the best features of both. Built of stucco in a Spanish adobe style, the complex of buildings opened in 1923. Beyond a triumphal entry arch was a recreation hall, 66 by 20 feet, with a community kitchen and dining hall at the rear of the building. Also on the grounds were a gas station, grocery store, drug store, and souvenir shop.

But most interesting of all was the variety of sleeping accommodations offered to the tourist at Camp Grande. Out back there were campsites for rent. On Rustic Row the camper could rent a covered space beneath a continuous pine log roof structure. Or the visitor could opt to rent tourist cabins of various types and sizes called "bungalettes." The smaller ones were one-bedroom units with bath and kitchenette, while the larger cabins had additional sleeping rooms, living room, and breakfast room.

KORONADO KOVRTS
ON HIGHWAY 66
WEST OF MAIN STREET
JOPLIN, MISSOURI

A grand array of tourist facilities were offered along U.S. 66, and they were positively portrayed on this foldout postcard. The Koronado was described as "the finest and most up-to-date tourist kourts in the entire Southwest."

A highly ornate entrance arch was used to entice the passing parade to stop and spend the night at Swanson's Cabin Camp in Chamberlin, South Dakota.

Cabin camps proliferated quickly, and as at Camp Grande, private enterprise had stepped in to reap the rewards. By 1925 Florida had some 178 of these new roadside businesses that, five years before, had scarcely existed. Another source estimates that there were some 1,000 cabin camps in the United States in 1920, and that this number had doubled by 1926.

But Camp Grande notwithstanding, and not even this camp was all that grand, the choice of where to spend the night was usually limited to "shacks with spigot" camps. A 1929 article in *National Petroleum News* reported that most gas station operators got into the tourist cabin business by throwing up a few cabins on one or two acres, and considered them to be "rustic affairs." The cabins were usually provided with only a few essentials: electric light, gas heat, and water under pressure.

Extremely humble homes on the range were offered at the Cactus Motel in Zapata, Texas, not far from Laredo.

A visible gas pump promised plenty of fuel at Hudson's Camp. The cabins appear to have been "cozy" at best.

33

A well-traveled family has just arrived at a tourist cabin in the Adirondack Mountains in New York State, circa 1930.

A larger than average cabin camp in 1929 was operated by a Mrs. D. J. Flannigan on the south edge of Macon, Georgia. On an acre beside a gas station were 23 cabins renting from $1 to $1.50 a night (the cheapest hotel in town was $2.50 a night). Each unit had a private adjoining garage, two iron beds with springs and mattresses (linens supplied upon request), two chairs, a table, a dresser, and a stove for cooking or heating. In a separate building were a bathhouse and laundry, and another structure housed a grocery store fully stocked with foods and merchandise.

By 1935, in another article in *National Petroleum News*, cabin camps were described as being of two types — the $1 cabin and the 50-cent cabin. The dollar cabins weren't all that bad: a bed with good springs, lavatory, toilet, tub or shower, chairs, lamp, and many had interior walls. There was usually a restaurant or a kitchen in a separate building, and some operations even had a swimming pool. The 50-cent cabin was much

A clapboard twin cabin at the Winnibigoshish Resort along Highway 2 in Bena, Minnesota, 1933, is 25 by 15 feet in size, and is dazzling to the eye with its freshly painted red and green trim. In 1980 this entire motor court complex was placed on the National Register of Historic Places.

The Mountain Terrace Motel, located one-half mile west of the Bagnal Dam in Lake Ozark, Missouri, offers handsome cabins sheathed and embellished with contrasting-colored stonework.

In the 1930s a cluster of little cabins, not immodestly called "Paradise," were described as being located in New York City. Actually they were in the distant borough of the Bronx, quite a bit more than a hop, skip, and a jump from Radio City and the Empire State Building.

The miniature-golf-like profile of this unit at Marteen's Cabins in Marlboro, New York, was not achieved by structural integrity but by decorative wood appendages to an otherwise conventional rectangular building.

more spartan, offering little more than a bed with bathroom facilities and electricity, and a lunch-counter-type eating facility. Even so, James Agee, in his 1934 article in *Fortune,* could wax poetic about "the oddly excellent feel of a weak-springed mattress in a clapboard transient shack."

In the same article, Agee described in detail an even nicer two-dollar cabin: "In this one you find a small, clean room, perhaps ten by twelve. Typically its furniture is a double bed—a sign may have told you it is Simmons, with Beautyrest mattress — a table, two kitchen chairs, a small mirror, a row of hooks. In one corner a washbasin with cold running water; in another the half-opened door to a toilet. There is a bit of chintz curtaining over the screened windows, through which a breeze is blowing....Inside you have just what you need for a night's rest, neither more nor less. And you have it with a privacy your hotel could not furnish — for this night this house is your own."

In less than 15 years a bunch of shacks had evolved into a national institution. With millions of people and cars taking to the road, the tourist cabin business grew into a large industry. By the 1930s the boom was on. One source estimated there were 9,848 tourist courts in 1935, increasing 39 percent to 13,521 by 1939, with total motor court registrations pre—Pearl Harbor at some 225 million.

Hotel owners nationwide, alarmed by this new and sometimes substandard competition, lobbied various levels of government to regulate or even abolish the cabin trade. But this strategy backfired, and instead of causing the competition to go away, it caused cabin camps to upgrade and expand their facilities—creating even more competition for the hotels marooned in downtowns. In 1940 *Business Week* cited additional statistics that were more bad news for the hotel industry: An AAA survey of its membership showed that in 1937, 61 percent of its members stayed at hotels while only 12.5 percent stayed at courts. Just two years later, hotel preference had slipped to 46 percent while motor court patronage had more than doubled to 28 percent.

By the early to middle 1930s deluxe cabins began to appear, more substantially constructed and supplied with heating so that they could operate year-round. Better-quality restaurants were built near the cabin courts. Much of this new quality expansion was concomitant with the re-routing of highways around the outskirts of town, thereby creating new, spacious sites developed into automotive strips. Cabin camps evolved into "tourist courts" as the units were arranged around a common lawn area or "court" reminiscent of bungalow colony facilities at resorts or apartment courts in places like Southern California and Florida. The lawn or court was often embellished with lawn furniture, playground equipment for the kids, and even swimming pools. Some cabin camps were unusually elegant and luxurious. Several references speak of the "ultimate perfection" of super cabin camps in California that combined the features of the auto camp with the amenities of a hotel. There were very large ones in Los Angeles and Fresno, and the Venetian Court in Long Beach reportedly cost $500,000 to build and charged guests an unheard of eight dollars a night to stay in one of its 200 units.

Twin-gabled bliss complete with a private fire-place for those chilly nights is offered at Hearthside Village, a vacationer's Eden in the White Mountains at Littleton, New Hampshire.

Rusticated local stone was used to construct the Rock Cabin Court in Eureka Springs, Arkansas. The tourist complex has updated its function and it now operates a bed-and-breakfast facility.

Merl and Eunice Fernholz are justly proud of their immaculately maintained Fairyland Cottages in Detroit Lakes, Minnesota, which were built in the late 1930s. Each of the 13 cabins is decorated with a wooden cutout of a fairy-tale personage. The perfect line of pairs of red lawn chairs is the stuff that dreams are made of.

The Danish Village was built along U.S. 1 in Scarborough, Maine, designed by a Danish American architect who wished to "bring the old world to New England." Five structures of interconnected rooms were located around a town square with a central fountain topped by a statue of Niels Ebbenson, a Danish patriot of the fourteenth century.

California was not alone. A Danish village confection was build along U.S. 1 in Scarborough, Maine, just south of Portland, in 1929. Henry P. Rines, who had built the $2 million dollar Eastland Hotel in Portland in 1927, saw a need for a high-class roadside facility in the area, and he chose as his architect Peter Holdensen, a Danish American who had created the Danish Tea Room at the Eastland. Holdensen persuaded Rines to "bring the old world to New England" and decided to model the roadside hostelry after the medieval Danish village of Ribe.

Bedrooms at the Danish Village (178 of them) rented for $1.50 and were located in half-timbered "house" units that sometimes defined medieval-style crooked streets. The establishment, it was said, was for "the better class of the motoring public," including First Lady Eleanor Roosevelt, who once spent a night here on her way to Campobello.

Each of the Grandview Cabins in Holyoke, Massachusetts, was named for a different state denoted on a sign beneath the cross-hatched gabled entranceway, as seen in this real-photo postcard. The entrance signage to the establishment, seen in a 1941 Farm Security Administration photograph, doesn't look all that different from motel signs of the 1950s and 1960s, except that a dinner of chicken and spaghetti would no longer cost a mere 50 cents.

By the early 1940s the business of housing transients had proven itself to be Depression-proof. And with 25 million cars on the road and new motor courts being built at the rate of 800 per year, there seemed to be no end to the tourist court boom. A roadside housing survey published by the advertising agency Young & Rubicam showed clearly how advanced the state of the art had become in 1940: 87 percent of the rooms had private baths, 89 percent had heating, 14 percent had air conditioning, 72 percent provided innerspring mattresses, 60 percent had rugs or carpeting, and 16 percent had room phones.

39

Bidgood's GLEN
HORTON-N.Y.

As the motel business boomed, at least some establishments began to have a sleazy image, and not undeservedly so. Criminals would use the cabins as the perfect hideouts, some became ideal venues for houses of prostitution, and even otherwise model citizens would meet surreptitiously in cabins buried beneath the trees for trysts and other brief encounters of passion. Some establishments across the country even came to call themselves "no-tell motels."

But such aberrations notwithstanding, the American motor court had come of age and had become the facility of choice for tourists on the move. In the next decades, as the institution of the motel became even more popular, the roadside facilities would become even more sophisticated and deluxe. The big losers were the downtown hotels, which lost their customers, and with them much of their very reason to be in business at all.

A picturesque line of tiny cabins nestled in the shade were a beckoning sight to passersby on the southern edge of the Catskill Mountains in New York State.

Littlefield's Ogunquit Camps
Ogunquit, Maine

This extraordinary aerial photograph of Littlefield's Ogunquit Camps shows it to be a veritable tourist city by the sea. At least 100 cabins of various sizes were available for rent.

BAKEN TOURIST CAMP
RAPID CITY S.DAK.
"IN THE BLACK HILLS."

LOG CABINS

The log cabin has long symbolized the spirit of pioneering in the growth of the United States. It isn't surprising, therefore, that tourist cabin owners adopted this building form along the highways and byways of America. Looking a lot like the Lincoln Log toys of our youth, these structures projected just the right kind of image to attract tourists. As the spirit of automotive adventuring faded and interstate uniformity homogenized the roadside environment, so too did the romantic notion of cabins in and of the woods. Today this once-common wayside dwelling is a seldom-seen artifact.

Montrose, Colorado

The Log Cabin Tourist Camp along the postal highway (which became U.S. 66) seemed like a fitting place for two tribes to hold a powwow in 1925. Advertisements for the Log Cabin Park offered: "fellowship treatment, oodles of shade, rest-rooms—all free. Shower baths for the entire family, 25 cents."

An aura of rustic serenity prevailed at Mr. Lackey's cabins beside a major north-south highway in Virginia.

Logs extending beyond the corner notching create a lattice-like pattern in one unit at the Tawas Inn Cabins in East Tawas City, Michigan.

Horizontal and vertical patterns of logs and chinking created a rough-hewn environment at a log cabin lunchroom, location unknown, probably dating from the late 1930s.

The sublime and imposing Morro Bay Rock looms beyond a conjoined line of rooms at the Log Cabin Motel in Morro Bay, California.

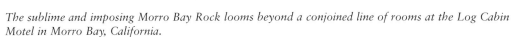

SLEAZEBO MOTELS

In the business of accommodating tourists not everything was peaches and cream. While tourist cabins proved to be an ideal solution for travelers seeking a place to rest their head along their journey, some of these very same places earned an unsavory reputation as the venues of choice for those with less than honorable intentions. Corny jokes abounded: What is motel spelled backwards? Letom. Kids turn into teenagers, but what do teenagers turn into? Motels. Colloquial terms such as "hot sheet" motel, "hot pillow joints," and "Mr. and Mrs. Jones" motels came into common usage.

As early as 1928 there are documented instances of referral chains reacting to the seamier side of serving transients. "Beware of the disreputable roadhouse," warned the Yellow Octagon Guide. "Places which tolerate drinking parties or maintain public dance halls of the questionable type, have no place in the 'Approved Wayside Stations.'"

In a study undertaken by the Sociology Department at Southern Methodist University in 1935 and published in their scholarly journal in 1936, teams

Camps of CRIME

Behind many alluring roadside signs are dens of vice and corruption, says America's head G-Man . . . He points out the menace to the public from hundreds of unsupervised tourist camps, 1940-style hideaways for public enemies

of students were dispatched to determine "the function and significance of the urban tourist camp." Using subterfuge, pairs of student investigators would check into cabins and check out the action. License plate numbers were recorded, and the numbers of couples checking in and out were duly observed. Their conclusions about one of the locations were applicable to nearly all of the tourist cabin camps in the study: "This tourist camp is no resting place for the weary, but is an abode of love, a bower of bliss in which amorous couples devote themselves to the worship of Venus."

Some of the statistical information obtained about these camps is staggering to the imagination. In one four-cabin camp patronized in a 10-day period by 109 couples from the city of Dallas (and by 145 other couples as well), 102 of them gave fictitious names and addresses. In one camp a proprietor reported that he had turned over a single cabin 16 times on one Saturday. Quotes from other camp owners were equally revealing: "Ninety per cent of my customers use the cabins for immoral purposes," said one, while another explained, "We can't rent to tourists on week-ends or busy nights because it would ruin our couple trade."

DRAWING BY
STEVAN DOHANOS

Stevan Dohanos

J. Edgar Hoover himself attacked the tourist camp industry with a lurid exposé in The American Magazine *in 1940. Hoover's article was accompanied by an ethereal and haunting illustration by Stevan Dohanos that subtly captured the redolence of a roadside dive.*

Of course some motel owners in the Dallas area, as well as others across the country, wanted nothing whatsoever to do with such goings on, and hence the meaning of the admonition "tourists only" became entirely clear. At one motel near Roanoke, Virginia, Traveltown No. 1, a source reported that admittance was refused to "suspicious" couples and to all couples with license plates that could be determined to have come from within a 50-mile radius of the motel.

At the height of this moralistic craze, no less than the likes of J. Edgar Hoover wrote a lurid and sensational article, "Camps of Crime," in *The American Magazine* in February 1940. Hoover said that behind many alluring roadside signs are dens of vice and corruption, that "assignation camps are closed to the traveling public on Saturdays and Sundays," and that "marijuana sellers have been found around such places." Hoover's basic thesis is summarized in one paragraph from the article: "The facts are simple. A majority of the 35,000 tourist camps throughout the United States threatens the peace and welfare of the communities upon which

Dick Tracy knew a good hideout when he saw one as he raided a tourist camp in a comic strip from 1950.

Comic postcard from the 1960s.

One branch of the Wigwam Village motel chain in Rialto, California, built with naïveté and good intentions in the early 1950s, had lost its frontier charm by the middle 1970s when it began to invite passersby to "do it in a tee pee." In 1991 the back of its business card offered such amenities as mirrored rooms, XXX movies, and hourly rates of (as was hand-written in) $15 and up.

these camps have fastened themselves and of all of us who form the motoring public. Many of them are not only hideouts and meeting places, but actual bases of operation from which gangs of desperados prey upon surrounding territories."

But high-minded moral indignation notwithstanding, people would do what they would do, and they still do. When we notice signs posted outside of contemporary motels advertising "day rates" and "hourly rates," it doesn't take much imagination to figure out what's going on inside.

Chapter 4

Anatomy of a Motel

LET'S SWIM

With the evolution of places to stay beside the road, a new vocabulary of design elements evolved as well. Signs, offices, lobbies, restaurants, bedrooms, and recreational facilities, in their translation to the roadside, had to take on new forms and variation. The people who built and operated cabin camps and motels were quite aware of the decision faced by their potential clientele each night as they sped by. Many of these entrepreneurs, at least many of the shrewder of them, designed their establishments to be as alluring as possible.

A bikinied orange brontosaurus sign is an invitation for tourists to take the plunge at the Best Western Antlers Motel in Vernal, Utah, the dinosaur hot spot of the U.S.A.

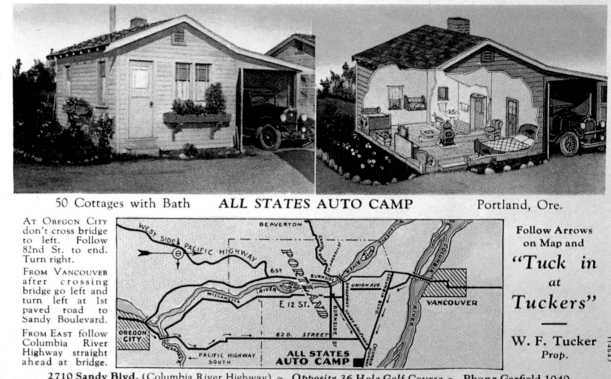

50 Cottages with Bath **ALL STATES AUTO CAMP** Portland, Ore.

AT OREGON CITY don't cross bridge to left. Follow 82nd St. to end. Turn right.

FROM VANCOUVER after crossing bridge go left and turn left at 1st paved road to Sandy Boulevard.

FROM EAST follow Columbia River Highway straight ahead at bridge.

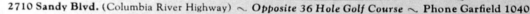

Follow Arrows on Map and

"Tuck in at Tuckers"

W. F. Tucker Prop.

2710 Sandy Blvd. (Columbia River Highway) ∿ **Opposite 36 Hole Golf Course** ∿ Phone Garfield 1040

W. F. Tucker bared all in order to attract guests to his auto camp in Portland, Oregon. The cutaway view of the cabin showed an elaborately furnished 1920s-style sleeping room.

The floor plan of a particularly luxurious cabin at the Utah Motor Court in Salt Lake City in 1931 shows a cottage with a kitchen, dining area, two lavatories, and many sleeping choices, including a clever disappearing bed in the living room.

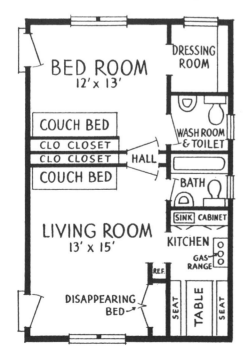

First impressions were what it was all about: where the business was located and sited, and what motorists could see from behind the wheel through their windshield. Attractively maintained landscaping, flower beds, a fresh coat of paint, even a swimming pool (a seductive-looking but seldom used facility) — all such cosmetic amenities and more helped to bring tourists to a halt.

A new ritual evolved as the traveler made his important nightly decision. James Agee, in his 1934 *Fortune* article, describes the process with his usual poetic clarity: "It is six in the afternoon and you are still on the road, worn and weary from three hundred miles of driving. Past you flashes a sign

DE LUXE CABINS ONE MILE....And around the next bend set back amid a grove of cool trees you see the little semicircle of cabins which the sign warned you of. You pull in by a farmhouse — or a filling station, or a garage — which registers instantly as the mother hen to the brood.

"If you are a novice the routine is so simple as to take your breath away. The farmer or the filling station proprietor or either's daughter appears, puts a casual foot upon the runningboard, and opens the negotiations with a silent nod. You say 'How much are your cabins?' He or she says 'Dollar a head. Drive in by No. 6' He or she accompanies you, riding with the ease of habit on the

27 APARTMENTS—COMPLETELY FURNISHED—STEAM HEATED

LIVING ROOM—COMPLETELY CARPETED FLOORS

BEDROOM "BEAUTYREST" MATTRESSES AND ACE SPRINGS

KITCHEN—FRIGIDAIRE AND HOT POINT RANGE

BATHROOM—CRANE FIXTURES—BATH TUB, SHOWER

MOUNTAIN VIEW AUTO COURT

PHONE 4416   563 WEST TWENTY-FOURTH   OGDEN, UTAH

4A-H1202

Many aspects of the Mountain View Auto Court, Ogden, Utah, are seen here in a vintage postcard with a bird's-eye view of the entire layout and vignettes displaying its very up-to-date 1930s interior appointments. The entire complex was placed on the National Register of Historic Places in 1987.

The bridal suite at The Westerner Motor Hotel in Arcadia, California, was everything that a newlywed couple on the road could possibly hope for in the late 1940s. The furniture in the living room would fetch a hefty price in today's antiques market, and the draped-off bedroom chamber attempts to be discreet.

side of your car. You make your inspection. You do not commit yourself — as you do in a hotel — until you see your room. If you don't like it, you drive on — to the next cabin camp."

On the following pages are a gallery of motel facilities encompassing the key elements in any such establishment: offices and lobbies, pools and patios, restaurants, and guest rooms. All of them — the good, the bad, and the ugly — were and are calculated to make James Agee, you, or me stop and spend a night of peaceful sleep and relaxation. The choice is ours to make.

BRIDAL
SUITE
at
*The
Westerner*

Southern
California's
Finest New
Motor Hotel

¼ Mile from
Santa Anita
Golf Course on
U. S. Highway 66

**ARCADIA
CALIFORNIA**

E3933

51

Offices & Lobbies

In the old days there were no public spaces in tourist courts, at least not interior public spaces. The "halls," "lobbies," and "meeting rooms" were the great outdoors — the lawns and woods surrounding the dwelling units. Very often there were also no offices with a registration desk; owners would pop out of their houses and negotiate in the driveway. Later on, small office structures were built or carved out of a small area in the owner's house. But as cabins evolved into motels, roadside hostelries incorporated many of the facilities that had formerly been offered only in the old downtown hotels. The structures and interior spaces shown here are but a few examples of motels shifting into a hotel mode.

The Host Ways Motel office points heavenward with ecclesiastical fervor to draw them off the interstate in East Haven, Connecticut.

It is likely that the owners of Ann's Motel in Barre, Vermont, didn't want strangers trudging in and out of their home, and so this tiny structure was probably built to check 'em out as they checked in.

The cabins were gone and the office was barely still there in 1980 along Highway 31 in Manistee, Michigan. By the late 1980s, not a trace was to be seen.

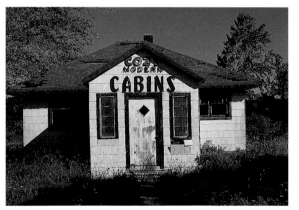

The check-in desk and lobby area of the Bel-Air Motel had all of the idiosyncracies and clutter of an individually owned and operated business.

The lounge was a latecomer to roadside establishments as motels became motor hotels after World War II. The lobby at the Motel El Corral in Tucson, Arizona, was a handsome space to wait around in, with its brightly colored furniture, Western art, and cacti, which brought the outside inside.

The office at the Rock Log Motel in Glendive, Montana, is a marvel of vernacular design—immaculately maintained and with a rusted wagon wheel partially buried out front as a decorative lure.

53

Pools & Patios

Although there are references to the existence of swimming pools at the roadside as early as the 1920s, the idea didn't really catch on until the 1930s. And after World War II a motel pool was de rigueur. The irony in all of this was that these concrete oceans were seldom used. Their real function was symbolic; they were a visible icon used to make potential customers stop. Certainly many kids would hop into their suits and jump in. But most adults didn't bother or knew better, steering clear of these cauldrons of chlorine and urine. What was important about the pools, patios, and surrounding landscaping is that they represented a taming and refinement of the landscape as the motel building type became more refined and sophisticated.

In this idyllic portrait of motel facilities along old Highway 80 in Jackson, Mississippi, in 1979, a dreamy pool edged by rainbow-hued metal deck chairs is dwarfed by the large and fabulous Flamingo Motor Hotel sign. Everything here had vanished by the middle 1980s.

In this charming magazine advertising illustration for Quality Courts in 1962, the entire family is about to be cooled off instantly, presumably after a hot day's drive.

A swan-diving woman attired in a two-piece bathing suit and a bathing cap was the classic symbol used to denote the Fresno Motel in Fresno, California.

HOLLYWOOD STAR MOTEL. 5270 SUNSET BLVD., HOLLYWOOD. CALIF.

Inexpensive reclining tubular lawn furniture never looked any better than it did here on the sun patio at the Hollywood Star Motel on Sunset Boulevard in Hollywood, California.

Tallahassee Motor Hotel and Lake Ella Motor Court Swimming Pool

Throngs were in attendence in and beside a pool with water so exotically and artificially blue that it might just have been ladled out of the Caribbean and imported to Tallahassee, Florida.

55

The Motel Restaurant

Early on, municipal and private auto camps offered communal kitchens. And many of the early tourist cabins had kitchenettes that were sometimes supplied by small grocery stores on the premises. But sleepy Americans were also hungry Americans, and it didn't take most motel owners long to figure out that a restaurant added profits to their businesses — not only from people spending the night but from passersby as well as local clientele. These eating spots and watering holes took on many forms — from the simple lunchroom serving short-order fare to snazzy inns and nightclubs offering full-course meals, potent potables, and even live musical entertainment and dance halls. Any or all of these options were tempting food for thought for tourists seeking an ideal way station.

MOTEL RESTAURANT

Waitresses pose as they await hungry travelers at a prototypical motel restaurant next to Yendes' Motel on U.S. 40 in Vandalia, Ohio.

The Phillips Tourist Tavern, a "model tourist city" seen in this matchbook cover view, opened in 1933 in Excelsior Springs, Missouri. In addition to the tavern were eight cabins and a gas station—all in the "English cottage style" and distinctive orange and green coloration used by the Phillips Petroleum Company for its roadside buildings. At the opening dinner, guests were treated to such epicurean delights as "'Fill Up With Phillips' Appetizer A La Natural"; "Fried 'Phillips Fliers' with Cream Gravy 'Special Viscosity'"; and, finally, "Coffee— Iced Tea—Buttermilk 'Controlled Viscosity' 'Via Pipe Line.'"

Webbies Drive-In was the
restaurant for the Roselawn Court.

John Holiday offers room service
at Holiday Inn.

A humble lunchroom and
roadside stand located adjacent
to a tourist home in New Haven,
New York, were no doubt serving
very basic American cuisine.

The Motel Guest Room

Putting aside all of the other frills and amenities offered to the traveling public, the most vital part of any motel was the bedroom itself—the place where sleep loss would hopefully be replenished. But these "homes away from home"—the tourist's private space—had surprisingly little in common with the bedroom in one's own house. Yes, both had beds, but roadside mattresses varied considerably in quality, from firm and comfy to a nightmare of lumpy mashed potatoes long since pummeled into submission by 1,001 nights of tossing and turning. Early "shack and spigot" cabin furnishings were often no more than a bed, table, lamp, and chair. But as the art was perfected, the motel room evolved into a tone poem of shag carpets, indestructible furniture, indescribably predictable "great" art on the walls, and a heady aroma somewhere between eau de new car and Lysol wafting about the room. And occasionally there was that fabulous but elusive motel room nearly as sumptuous and comfortable as the one at the Palace or the Plaza.

beautifully furnished!

Enjoy the finest accommodations when you visit Reno. Rates are astonishingly low. Everything is new, modern, and beautifully planned for comfort. Deep carpeting, modern furniture, the best in bedding and inner-springs, electric heat, and a location just off the busy highway for restful quiet! First class room service. You'll be proud to entertain your Reno friends in these fine rooms. Individual garages are available with most rooms and suites.

Every room with telephone, radio, and bath.

For reservations telephone Reno 5-8316

Harolds Pony Express Motels proclaimed its rooms "beautifully furnished!" as they were being admired by a tourist couple in this circa-1950 brochure illustration. Every room, we are told, has a telephone, a radio, and a bath.

The room was cozy (i.e., small), but with its wood paneling and oodles of furniture it appeared to be a pleasant place to spend the night on Highway 66 in Albuquerque, New Mexico.

DAVIS AUTO COURT 2102 W. CENTRAL ON HIGHWAY 66, ALBUQUERQUE, N.M.

A dream chair and a brightly decorated chenille bedspread were the prominent features of this postcard detail view of a room at Halford's Court in Fort Stockton, Texas.

The Peach Springs, Arizona, Auto Court room had glossy enamel on the walls and linoleum on the floor. In 1974, its bed was a horror to behold.

A room at Durham's Deluxe Motel in Marysville, Washington, would have been a pretty nice place to stay in the late 1930s. And it was the photographer's pleasure to be able to line up this shot so that the vanity mirror captured even more of the interior environment.

BELIEVE IT OR NOT!

GREETINGS FROM THE BIGGEST COUPLE
MR. & MRS. FISCHER
WITH THE GREATEST SHOW ON EARTH

Motel owners were all selling the same product — a pied-à-terre to soothe weary motorists en route. But since human creativity knows no bounds, nearly anything is possible if not probable (even if entirely improbable) in motel design. Adding the profit motive to this equation, the individuals who constructed their businesses beside the road over the years have come up with flabbergasting schemes that stretch the very limits of our imagination. The buildings themselves are sometimes bizarre, and the materials used to construct them could occupy new niches in the annals of architectural history. In other places the owners have capitalized upon their own persona or sense of humor. The accommodations of renown shown here are a sideshow of delights; commercial ingenuity knows no bounds. Believe it or not!

Mr. and Mrs. Fischer, proclaimed as "the biggest couple with the greatest show on earth" in a promotional postcard, also owned the Pioneer Apartments in Sarasota, Florida, with overnight rooms for rent. This made them the largest mom-and-pop motel operators.

The miniature capitol at the Capitol Court on Highway 40 in Denver, Colorado, was certainly a wonder to behold. It was an exact replica of the state capitol building, built at a scale of one-half inch to the foot. Perhaps even more astounding, as related in information provided on the back of this postcard, is that this creation was planned and constructed in one year by a man with one hand.

At any conventional tourist court, the restaurant was usually a straightforward architectural statement. But at the Sunset Village just north of Lewisburg, Pennsylvania, in the 1930s, short-order fare and probably the best java in town were dished out from Betty's Coffee Pot, a percolator extraordinaire.

What's going on here? The office for this log cabin motel in San Leandro, California, isn't shaped like a little log cabin; it's shaped like a windmill. Will wonders never cease.

Perhaps the eighth wonder of the world were the 22 wine casks converted into tourist cabins along Lake Erie in Vermilion, Ohio, in 1928. The cabins at the Cask Villa were 7,800-pound oak vats purchased from a local winery, with porches added on in front, and two windows punched through the back for a view of the lake. Inside were a double folding bed, a folding table with benches, and a trap door in the center of the floor for storage of suitcases and other belongings.

In the land of big trees north of San Francisco, California, giant sequoias were hollowed out and turned into tourist oddities such as log houses, gift shops, and even a gas station. At Lane's Redwood Flat, a redwood tree became the registration office for tourist cabins beneath still-living trees.

Petrified wood, we are told, took millions of years before it became rock solid and termite-proof. So it isn't surprising that the Rock-Wood Motel on the northern edge of Klamath Falls, Oregon—built from these fossils as a labor of love by a folk artist over 50 years ago—has lasted longer than the highway on which it was built. Old Highway 97 has been totally eclipsed by the new bypass, denying most tourists the chance to behold or maybe even spend a night in this architectural tour de force.

Ho-Hum Motel
Burlington, Vt.

The Movie Manor Motor Inn was built as a broad V-shaped building with motel room picture windows looking away from the magnificent Rocky Mountain scenery in Monte Vista, Colorado. Instead, George Kelloff chose to direct the views to a drive-in movie screen, with sound controls in each room. Inside the rooms was a disclaimer that warned the guests who might be offended by what was on the screen to draw the drapes and do something else. Most, however, chose to watch the movies and eat popcorn supplied by the management.

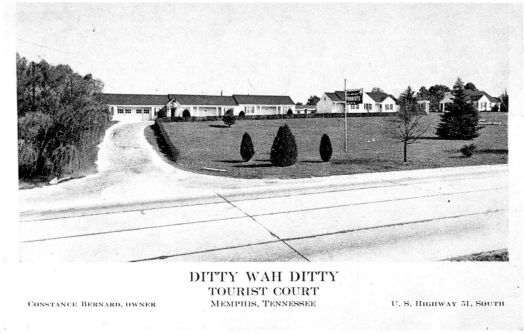

DITTY WAH DITTY
TOURIST COURT
CONSTANCE BERNARD, OWNER   MEMPHIS, TENNESSEE   U. S. HIGHWAY 51, SOUTH

Among the all-time greatest names in all of moteldom are the Ditty Wah Ditty Tourist Court and the Ho-Hum Motel. The Ditty Wah Ditty name made some sense because it was located in one of the great jazz centers in the U.S.A. But the Ho-Hum was another matter, with a name so nondescript as to make tourists yawn. But then again, maybe that was the basic idea.

The DC-7 Steakhouse, said to have been the largest propeller-driven plane owned by Pan-Am, sat grounded incongruously beside the swimming pool at the Byron Inn, Byron, Georgia, in the late 1970s. Dining in a real airplane was an intriguing but not very practical idea because of space limitations. In 1990 the plane was disassembled and sold as scrap.

The courtesy car at the Best Western in Titusville, Florida, runs on gasoline, not rocket fuel. Its novel configuration is quite appropriate to the location of the motel near the Space Coast deep in the heart of NASA-land.

In the 1920s, an aircraft builder came up with an uplifting idea to build a zeppelin-shaped lunch-room at a tourist camp on the Lincoln Highway near Pittsburgh, Pennsylvania. In the 1950s, the wood-framed building, sheathed in aluminum, was moved to Rootstown, Ohio, where it once again served as a motel restaurant before it was converted into a private residence.

Chapter 5

Banding Together:
The Early Chains

Western's, I mean BEST **Western** MOTELS are always the best

W hatever the type of establishment that motel owners had to sell to the public, business strategies were devised to increase patronage. Two major methods were used to attract transient business: the referral chain, where independent owners would group together for their common good, and the franchised chain, a purer concept, where the idea was to build a series of identical lodging accommodations (some units were company-owned while others were farmed out). The premise led to the monoliths of today's lodging industry — Holiday Inn, Howard Johnson's, Ramada, Best Western, and the like.

66

California architect Robert B. Stacy-Judd, at the behest of a hotel chain, developed a prototype design for a series of Motel O'Rodomes in 1923—24, although this chain got no further than the drawing board. This project may well have been the first use of the term "motel." But most sources acknowledge that the first constructed example using this name was the Milestone Mo-Tel, which opened for business in December 1925, in San Luis Obispo, California, about halfway between Los Angeles and San Francisco. It was part of a plan for 18 Mo-Tels to be located about 150 to 200 miles apart between San Diego and Seattle, but only the one was ever built. The copyrighted words "Milestone" and "Mo-Tel" were the inspiration of another California architect and developer, Arthur S. Heineman. The San Luis Obispo Mo-Tel's highway facade was grandiose and eloquent, featuring a three-tiered bell tower modeled after the Mission in Santa Barbara. Heineman's mission-style hostelries strove to be an updated automotive equivalent to the historic missions of old California, where each was located a day's horseback ride apart along the El Camino Real.

The Mo-Tel was the creation of architect Arthur S. Heineman, who envisioned a lodging chain along the West Coast. Only one was ever built, shown here in a watercolor drawing and a photogaph from the 1970s. This claimant to the title of "first motel" opened in 1925 on Highway 101 in San Luis Obispo, California.

The Pierce Pennant Hotels from the 1920s were part of another grandiose roadside dream: to build identical, luxurious accommodations every 150 miles from New York to San Francisco. Five were built, and one survives to this day as the clubhouse for a retirement home in Columbia, Missouri. It has been placed on the National Register of Historic Places.

A perfectly nice cabin was prefabricated by Green Gable Camp Cottages, a small chain in the Midwest that failed to leave an indelible impression on the world.

TOURIST CABINS, TAVERNS FOR A COMPLETE CAMP

Sole Manufacturers of the National Advertised KOMFYKAMP Taverns and Kabins. The Log Cabin effect. Camp owners automatically become members of the KOMFYKAMP OWNERS' ASSOCIATION. For further information write the

HAWKEYE MANUFACTURING COMPANY, BELMOND, IOWA

Manufacturers of Portable, Ready Built Buildings.

Wayside Salesman, March, 1931

The Milestone Mo-Tel was quite luxurious for its time, and it cost $80,000 to build. The Spanish theme was carried through into its dining room, where great bunches of red peppers were hung from exposed beams and waitresses wore Spanish-style outfits—shiny white blouses, satin vests, and large hats bedecked with a red rose motif. The rooms, of various sizes, 40 in all, and each with a private garage, were situated around a court-yard and rented for a rather pricey sum of from $2 to $8.50 a night. The Mo-Tel, which became Motel Inn in its later years, still stands beside Highway 101 on the northern edge of San Luis Obispo. It has been closed for several years, but its new owner, Bob Davis, has visions of restoring it as a roadside museum.

Another grandiose idea for luxurious highway accommodations was hatched by Pierce Petroleum Corporation in 1929. Pierce constructed five "Terminals" in the southern Midwest at a cost of $2 million, and if all went well, they planned to build one every 150 miles all the way from New York to San Francisco.

A Pierce Pennant Terminal was a study in extravagance. On a 10-acre site with 600 feet of highway footage was a complex of buildings beyond a large neon sign: a filling station island and a building for auto repair and maintenance, a 40-room hotel to the rear with a "free" garage on its lower level, and a terminal building featuring a "soda fountain lobby" 501 feet long and 35 feet deep with a huge fireplace at one end. This building was decorated with a slew of Currier and Ives prints

ALAMO PLAZA COURTS

AMERICA'S FINEST

Dallas Highway - 1800 Block West Erwin

TYLER, TEXAS

ROOMS & APARTMENTS BY DAY OR WEEK
2 Persons $1.50 & $2.00

A BEAUTYREST MATTRESS On Every Bed
A Telephone In Every Room

PRIVATE TUB & SHOWER BATHS
Tile Floors

intermingled with other fine appointments. The bedrooms had, among other features, electric irons, folding ironing boards, and clothes dryers; deeply upholstered chairs; thickly-carpeted floors; "commodious clothes closets"; and French telephones.

But all did not go well. There wasn't a viable market for expensive roadside facilities. Pierce Petroleum and its hotels were bought by Sinclair, and the hotels lost money and flopped. But a Pierce Pennant Terminal built in Columbia, Missouri, still stands today as the Candle Light Lodge Retirement Center, and it was placed on the National Register of Historic Places in the early 1980s.

A much more humble chain of prefabricated cabins was promoted in a small, fascinating, but not well-known magazine called *Wayside Salesman* in March 1931. Green Gable Camp Cottages, made by a company in Onawa, Iowa, advertised: "Here's what a Green Gable franchise gives you — exclusive distinctive cottages, design patented... Road Signs. Advertising. Tourist good will. And big profits....Only one franchise given to a community. You are protected."

Probably not so coincidentally, an article-editorial matter ran in the very same issue of *Wayside Salesman* entitled, "Tourist Camps Prove Popular." This article about a Green Gable in Crookston, Minnesota, quotes a reporter from the local newspaper: "Stepping into a Green Gable cabin brings you a surprise. It is much larger than you would expect and instead of just an army cot and a camp stool there is a large Simmons double bed, Simmons mattress and Simmons springs, a square table, three benches, a wall mirror, two shelves and an electric plate for cooking. Never do we remember having seen

The Alamo Plaza Courts were probably the first successful national chain. The first one opened in Waco, Texas, in 1929, and then they began to spread. A typical example is shown here reproduced on a blotter. The premise of their signature building is unmistakable. By 1960, there were 34 Alamo Plazas.

The Alamo Plaza in Gulfport, Mississippi, was alive and well in 1980. Its Alamo shape is entirely frontal and skin deep — roadside artifice of the first order. Alamo-like shapes, alamo-ettes, are the facades for lines of rooms.

anything so complete and immaculate as these Green Gable cottages, both inside and out, and we aren't the only ones raving about the camp. Tourists have been filling these cabins every night since they have been put up." Since no other references have turned up about Green Gable, it can be assumed that the chain did not succeed.

The first successful motel chain was based upon the unforgettable premise of remembering the Alamo. The first Alamo Plaza Tourist Court opened in Waco, Texas, in 1929—a joint venture of Edgar Lee Torrance, who was in the automobile business, and Judge J. W. Bartlett. Torrance and Bartlett built the white-stucco facade of their drive-through office and registration structure so that it looked a lot like the Alamo in San Antonio. Others soon opened in various locations throughout the southern and

southwestern United States, some company-owned and others franchised, until there were a total of 34 Alamo Plazas by 1960. After that, the chain began to fall apart, a victim of the interstate highway system and the insurmountable competition of the new super-corporate giants like Holiday Inn. Today only a few Alamo Plazas cling to life along bypassed highways, still stunning in their old-fashioned theatrical roadside bravura.

By the late 1920s small groups of independent cabin owners formed associations that promised tourists-on-the-move certain predictable standards of quality and that served as a method to pass customers from one member of the organization to another. Unlike the Alamo Plazas, which had instantly recognizable and nearly identically shaped office structures, these "referral" chains adopted a common name and an official-

looking sign to identify themselves in addition to their own unique and specific identification. Brochures were printed and distributed free or for a nominal charge to travelers. Inside these pamphlets were short descriptions, often with key symbols, of the facilities offered in each place.

But the referral idea dates back at least to 1909, when a now defunct organization, the Automobile Club of America, had a very snazzy sign for its "officially appointed hotels." And constituent organizations of the American Automobile Association were recommending lodging at about the same time. The AAA guidebooks we know now began to evolve in the mid-1920s. And by the late 1920s, American oil companies, which certainly had an interest in keeping everyone rolling along, established travel bureaus to spread the word on "better" places to stay.

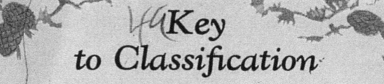

Key to Classification

BEST CAMPS does not undertake to distinguish between Wood, Stucco, Log or Brick buildings.

"Standard Equipment in Cabins consists of Beds, Springs, Mattresses, Mattress Covers, Chairs, Tables, Running Water, Sinks, Electric Lights, Heat and Cooking Devices."

A - 1 to 3 Rooms—Standard Equipment
AA - 1 to 3 Rooms—Standard Equipment with Addition of Private Bath and Toilet
AA* - 1 to 3 Rooms—Standard Equipment with Addition of Private Toilet
AA** - 1 to 3 Rooms—Standard Equipment with Addition of Private Bath
AAA - Same as AA but completely furnished with Bedding, Linen, Dishes, Cooking Utensils, etc.
AAA* - Furnished complete for Sleeping only with Private Bath and Toilets
A** - For Sleeping only (not furnished with Private Bath and Toilet)
B - 1 to 3 Rooms—Standard Equipment but without Running Water and Sink
B* - 1 Room for Sleeping only
BL - Bedding and Linen furnished upon request
CD - Cooking Utensils and Dishes furnished upon request
M - Meals furnished on Grounds
MB - Meals furnished nearby
TS - Tent Space
CK - Community Kitchen
CS - Community Showers
Sh - Trees large enough to afford Shade
St - Store—General Tourist Supplies, Fruit, etc.
SS - Service Station—Gas, Oils, Accessories
C - Confectionery—Soft Drinks, Ice Cream, etc.
GP - Greasing Pit
WR - Washing Rack
Gr - Garage
L - Laundry
SP - Swimming Pool
R - Radio in Cabins for Guests
MG - Midget Golf Course

TRAUNG LABEL CO. S.F. CALIF.

In the Best Camps brochure of the western states in 1931, everything was very complicated. A nearly endless array of amenities was listed, including "MG—Midget Golf," the latest and greatest craze of that time. Users of this guide would have had to plan ahead in order to cope with all of the alternatives available.

Commercial verses laud a long-forgotten motel chain, the National Tourist Association of Grand Rapids, Michigan, on the inside cover of an early 1930s brochure.

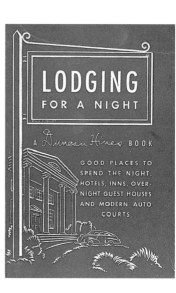

THE DUSTY TRAIL

As we travel o'er the dusty trail,
From preference by road instead
   of rail,

A haven we would like to see,
Where we may spend the night
   carefree.

An N. T. A. sign beckons us,
To a place that we can trust.

For "Supervised Service" has it
   under care,
We're sure of treatment fair and
   square.

Its homelike comfort keeps us well,
Where'er we stop we love to dwell.

The morning finds us on our way,
And at the end of our driving day

We again welcome the White-Green
   sign of N. T. A.

—A. Traveler.

Private individuals as well took it upon themselves to get out on the road to seek out and identify high-quality establishments. The most famous individual name in recommending good places to spend the night and great places to eat was Duncan Hines. Beginning in 1936 with his first culinary guidebook, *Adventures in Good Eating*, and in 1938 with his first *Lodging for a Night*, Mr. Hines issued annual listings of places that could post "Recommended by Duncan Hines" signs in front of their operations. Hines professed total independence and impartiality in compiling his lists. Motel

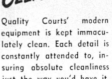

ENJOY A QUALITY COURT EVERY NIGHT!

CLEAN
Quality Courts' modern equipment is kept immaculately clean. Each detail is constantly attended to, insuring absolute cleanliness just the way you'd have it.

RESTFUL
Quality Courts are furnished for relaxing eye appeal and thoughtfully arranged for privacy—including important added comfort of the beds on which you sleep.

All members of Quality Courts and all members of Best Western will make prepaid reservations for you with any of the nearly 1,000 members in the two organizations.

RELAXING
Quietly, privately, you relax in the roomy comfort of your home-away-from-home. There's hot water for bathing, shaving . . . soft, clean towels . . . and, often, air conditioning.

SAFE
At Quality Courts you relax, knowing that here, for your personal security, is a safe environment for your entire family . . . because the highest standards are continually maintained by Quality Courts.

Stop at these emblems for fine accommodations

owners considered inclusion in Hines's book as the "top" mention they could receive. Hines did not charge hostelries for inclusion, and he refused all advertising. His income was derived from retail sales through national distribution, and the cost of *Lodging for a Night* was $1.50 a copy in the mid-1940s. And in case the name Duncan Hines still has a familiar ring to it, it's because it lives on to this day on the shelves of grocery stores as a brand name for cake mixes.

One of the most important of the early referral chains was United Motor Courts, a national nonprofit group that was founded in 1932, at which time it began to publish and distribute guidebooks. By 1946 it had grown to include 500 members in 32 states, Canada, and Mexico, and it published and distributed some 500,000 guidebooks in that year. One of the reasons for United Motor Courts' importance in the motel industry is that it became the springboard for two of the giants in today's lodging industry — Quality Inns and Best Western.

Quality Inns began in 1939 as Quality Courts when seven southern motel operators split off from United Motor Courts and joined together to print 10,000 copies of their own travel directory. By 1941 Quality Courts United, a nonprofit corporation, was formed, and a common symbol, a gold seal with a blue ribbon, was adopted along with qualification standards for membership. And in 1963 Quality Courts seized its identity and changed its structure to a for-profit company. Now it is part of a lodging conglomerate, Choice Hotels International, with seven lodging brand names and nearly 3,000 properties in the United States and Canada.

Inspired by the United Motor Courts guidebook, and interested in the concept that motel guidebooks be distributed by oil companies and automobile clubs, Merile K. Guertin, a motel owner from Long Beach, California, organized Best Western Motels in 1947. Guertin and 66 selected motel owners banded together to do their own advertising and to direct business from one

By the late 1950s the referral chains had it all figured out. Instead of those earnest and well-intentioned classifications of 1929, Quality Court's aproach was clear—simplification and standardization. Clean, restful, relaxing, safe.

to another. Guertin hit the road in 1947 or 1948 to find new members, and he inspected 507 motels as he drove 4,956 miles in 29 days. In 1948, 5 million Best Western guides were published. The Best Western chain spread from coast to coast, established common standards, and in 1962 adopted its famous crown sign. Today it is the world's largest chain of independently owned and operated motels and hotels, with about 2,000 properties in the United States and Canada.

The trend toward standardization and homogenization on a nationwide scale were now firmly in place. With the construction of the interstate highway system and the new facilities that were being built to serve these highways, sameness and dullness were about to become the norm.

COWBOYS

The American cowboy, and the legends and folklore invoked by this brave and romantic figure, is one of the most powerful icons along American highways. The archetypal symbolism of the cowpoke in full regalia—hat, boots, chaps, spurs—on his trusty steed, taming the Wild West, has been used to great advantage by motel owners seeking to cash in on travelers at the end of their trail. Beyond the sign itself, cliché cowboy references can pervade every aspect of such thematic motels. Western imagery, reinforced by Hollywood movies, fiction, and TV, is so pervasive that it has broken out of the geographic boundaries of the West to dominate the entire United States.

At the Westward Ho Motel in Grand Forks, North Dakota, Don Lindgren built a cowboy boot swimmin' hole that rivals Liberace's piano-shaped extravaganza in Palm Springs. The boot is 30 by 60 feet and is heated to an ever-pleasant 82 degrees.

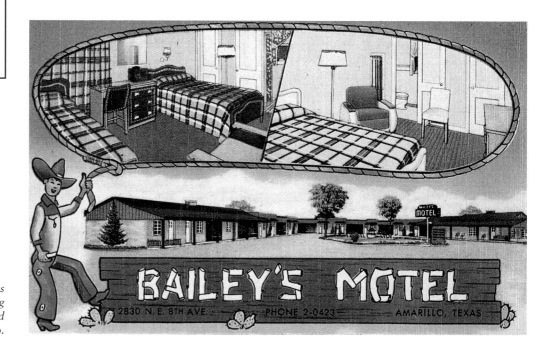

In this postcard for Bailey's Motel on Highways 60 and 66 in Amarillo, Texas, pleasant-looking rooms enlivened by Bates-like bedspreads and drapes are cordoned off by a giant lasso.

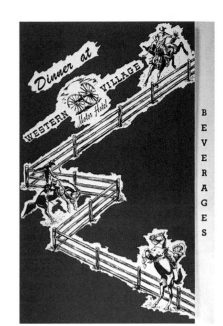

The ole corral fence and three cowboys on the hoof graced the dinner menu for folks looking for grub at the Western Village Motor Hotel in Phoenix, Arizona, in 1956.

A cowgirl, a rare species, cavorts on a hobbyhorse shown on a late-1940s brochure for the Ranch Motel in Laredo, Texas. The advertising copy chose food clichés to describe the atmosphere at the Ranch: "As western as pan-fried bread, wild pig steak and campfire coffee…yet tempered with an air of luxury one might expect to find in the most grand of haciendas."

A cowpoke leaning against a corral fence welcomes visitors on the outskirts of Wichita, Kansas.

INDIANS

The American Indian was every bit as potent an image as the cowboy — Tonto to the Lone Ranger in the ongoing adventure of the American road. At least this was true until recently, when a new sensitivity to Native Americans and their stereotyping in commercial advertising rendered such depictions politically incorrect, and rightly so. But in the heyday of the roadside, from the 1920s through the 1950s, the idea of the "noble savage" — chiefs, braves, squaws, and the symbols of their culture — was used to produce seductive advertising. The owners of roadside business didn't intend to insult anyone, but only to realize profits from their businesses. Masses of weary travelers made and stopped at roadside reservations to whoop it up, and then pull an Indian blanket over their heads before passing into that great dreamland in the sky.

An Indian brave statue looms above the Chieftain Motel in Carrington, North Dakota.

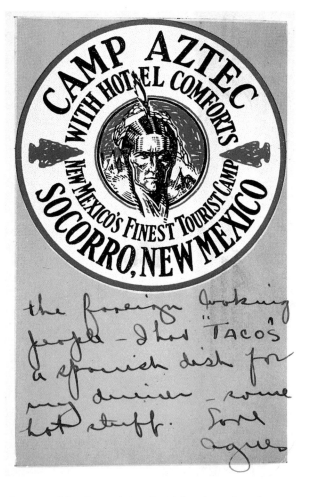

A postcard for Camp Aztec, "with hotel comforts," was sent by a man in 1930 after having just discovered that exotic culinary treat, the taco.

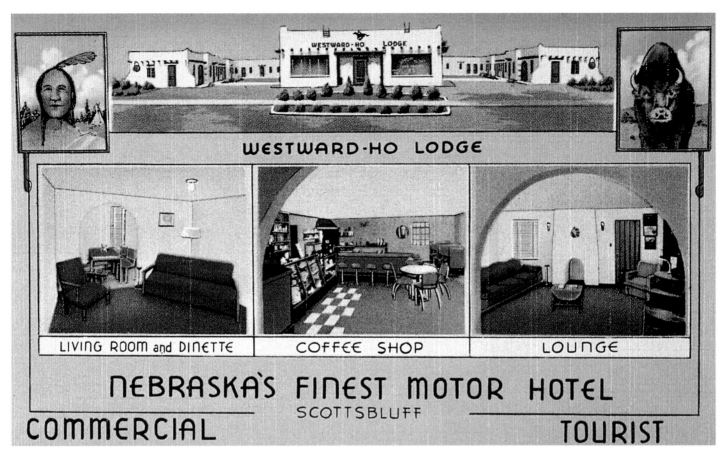

WESTWARD-HO LODGE

LIVING ROOM and DINETTE   COFFEE SHOP   LOUNGE

NEBRASKA'S FINEST MOTOR HOTEL
SCOTTSBLUFF

COMMERCIAL   TOURIST

*The Old West symbols of a brave and a buffalo were used
to enhance the postcard of the "Beautiful Westward-Ho,"
a pueblo-style motel with a full range of tourist facilities.*

*A scout on horseback served
as the beacon for the Lookout
Mountain Tourist Lodge in
Chattanooga, Tennessee.*

*An Indian in a brilliant full headdress graces the office sign
at the Chief Motel in Montrose, Colorado.*

WIGWAM MOTELS

Frank Redford, inspired by a teepee drive-in he had seen in California, patented his Wigwam Village cabin design in 1936.

Fig. 1

The strongest expression of the Indian theme wasn't the stereotypical representation of Native Americans themselves but rather the use of the teepee dwelling unit as the basis for tourist cabin design. A man named Frank Redford from Horse Cave, Kentucky, was the strongest player in the teepee motel business, founding his Wigwam Village chain there in 1931. Redford, who owned an ice-cream shop, had visited Long Beach, California, and, inspired by a teepee-shaped short-order food place he saw there on Third Street, returned home and opened a teepee restaurant with two smaller rest-room teepees on either side, one for "braves" and the other for "squaws."

Fig. 2.

A uniform patch and a sleeping room at Wigwam Village No. 2, Cave City, Kentucky.

Inventor

F. A. Redford

By *Clarence A. O'Brien* and *Hyman Berman* Attorneys

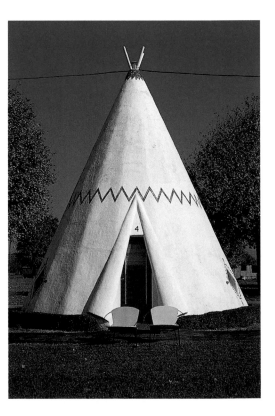

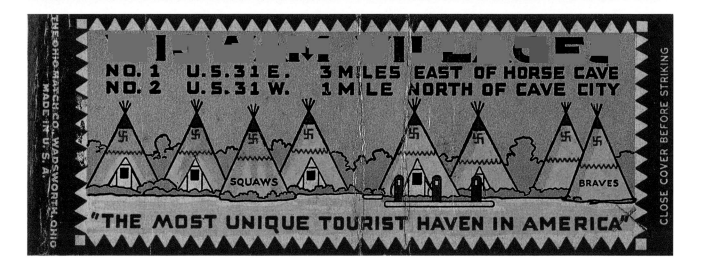

A splendid matchbook-cover view that advertised the first two Wigwam Villages showed the setup: an office-restaurant building with gas pumps out front, smaller rest-room teepees, and a bunch of tourist cabins. The Indian swastika symbol, borrowed and forever ruined by the Nazis, was painted out as World War II approached.

WIGWAM VILLAGE No. 4 — ORLANDO, FLORIDA

ORANGE BLOSSOM TRAIL, U. S. 441 AND U. S. 17; U. S. 92

8B-H528

A bird's-eye postcard view of Wigwam Village No. 4, a franchised unit in the chain of seven motels, shows a U-shaped village of 25 cabins deployed around a common lawn or "court."

Frank Redford totally understood the concept of roadside marketing through architecture. Make something large, outrageous, and unforgettable, and they will stop. The 24-hour restaurant was a huge success, and soon he built several teepee tourist cabins by the restaurant. He called them sleeping rooms and furnished them with hickory furniture and Indian rugs and decor. In 1935 he built a second Wigwam Village in nearby Cave City, Kentucky (both locations attracted tourists from the nearby Mammoth Cave), with 15 teepee rooms in a semicircle, a restaurant–gas station–gift shop, and smaller teepee rest-rooms. The formula was perfected and successful, and Redford patented his teepee cabin design.

Frank and Vetra Redford sold their Kentucky motels and moved to California after World War II. Wigwam Village No. 7, the last in the chain, was built in the early 1950s along Highway 66 in Rialto, California, just before it was bypassed by a freeway. Business was still brisk in the middle 1970s.

Vetra Redford, seen here in full Indian attire in the 1950s, although divorced from her husband, helped to run the family business in the late 1950s as Redford became increasingly ill.

Mr. Wigwam himself, Frank Redford, is seen here in his Seminole sweater in the 1930s.

The lunchroom in Cave City, Kentucky, described on the back of this postcard as "The Largest Wigwam in the World" (11 tons of steel and 37 tons of cement), was a beguiling and attractive assemblage of dining room and gift shop, along with a world-class Coke machine.

In the next 18 years, five more Wigwam Villages were constructed, four franchised operations in Bessemer, Alabama; New Orleans, Louisiana; Orlando, Florida; and Holbrook, Arizona, and the seventh and final one built by Redford himself in Rialto, California on Highway 66 in 1953 (Mr. Redford had sold his Kentucky motels in 1945). The Redford design patent notwithstanding (he never tried to enforce it), a whole slew of other wigwam motels sprang up throughout the United States and Canada. Frank Redford died in 1958 and the California motel was sold.

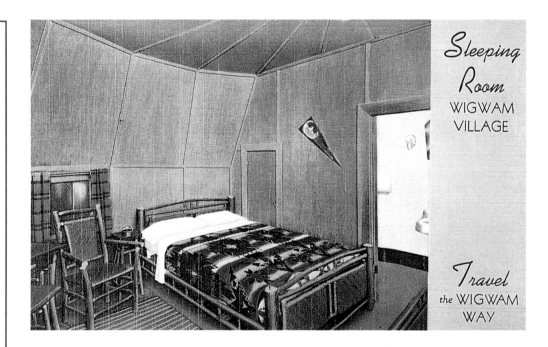

The postcard of the interior of a typical Wigwam "sleeping room" showed a snug ten-sided room with a dropped ceiling. A guest was treated to handsome furnishings including hickory furniture and an Indian blanket on the bed.

The Wigwam Lodge, Tempe, Arizona, offered unusual two-story teepees to tourists. The motel was once a larger group of buildings, but by the late 1970s only three remained, the rest having been razed to make way for a fast-food restaurant.

Redford's roadside entrepreneurship lives on to this day in the three units of his chain still operating in Cave City, Kentucky; Holbrook, Arizona; and Rialto, California. And a host of other motels with teepee cabins have come and gone. Two of them, the Wigwam Courts in Corsicana, Texas, and the DLD Motel in Hastings, Nebraska, have disappeared within the last decade. Politically correct or not, these roadside novelties captured the spirit and adventure of early American roadside culture.

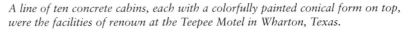
A line of ten concrete cabins, each with a colorfully painted conical form on top, were the facilities of renown at the Teepee Motel in Wharton, Texas.

The teepee motel phenomenon spread across the border to Canada. This cluster of cabins was probably located in the province of Quebec.

A teepee bedroom shown in the postcard view of the Indian Village on U.S. 1 in Virginia looked a lot like a Frank Redford model, but with the addition of an adjoining garage.

At least three Indian-style tourist cabins were part of an Indian Village tourist complex built in 1930 and 1931 by Frank W. McDonald on Highway 40 in Lawrence, Kansas. This group probably predated Frank Redford's Wigwam Village chain.

MOTEL BROCHURES

L ong ago, before there were 800 numbers and TV commercials, the motel brochure and guide was the major medium for motel owners to proclaim their establishments and to direct customers along from one location to the next. These brochures, distributed for free or at a minimal cost, featured covers that were sometimes distinctive and outstanding examples of commercial graphic art. In the late 1930s, United Motor Courts, then the largest nonprofit referral chain, issued a series of guides with colorful and elaborate cover art of idealized motel environments. In the 1940s it was Quality Courts that achieved eminence with its depictions of perfect tourist families stopping at glorious motels. The cover images shown on these pages represent the very best of this genre of advertising illustration. Like road maps, these motel guides are highly sought after by collectors of lasting evidence of the golden era of automotive adventure.

The 1931 brochure for "Best Camps" along the West Coast, unusual because of its expensive four-color printing, depicted a beautiful vision of a tourist cabin nestled within the natural splendor of a mountainous paradise. Most referral brochures of this era were little more than mimeographed lists.

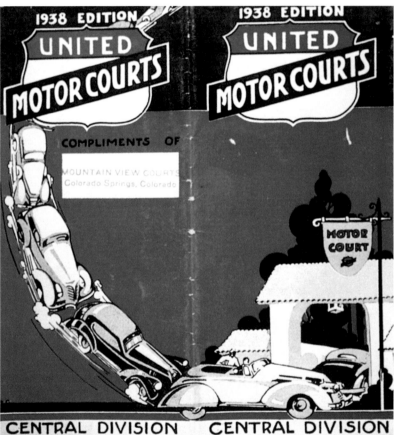

United Motor Courts was certainly the most important
and the largest referral chain in America, printing guidebooks said to have a circulation of 500,000 by 1946.
United Motor Courts brochure covers were among the
most attractive created in the late 1930s. The 1938 cover
(above, left) depicting a Streamline Moderne motel in
dazzling full color was the most spectacular of them all. But
a lot can also be said for the 1940 tourist court panorama
or the 1938 Central Division cover drawing of a line of
cars pulling off the highway and into a chosen court.

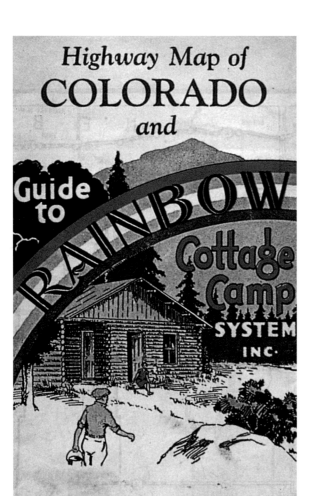

A strong black-and-white cover from the mid-1930s gave a clear view of the OK Auto Courts sign that could be found along the roads of the West Coast states.

The guide to the Rainbow Cottage Camp System, a midwestern chain from the late 1920s, was not elaborate graphically, but it provided a fully detailed state road map within.

The De Luxe brochure of 1940 showed a typical motor court, seen from above in this attractive drawing.

Ray A. Walker rated tourist facilities and published guidebooks for some 30 years. Most of the covers of his guide were drab productions in red, black, and white. His one winner was the 1940 Cabin Trails guide with a beaming typical family unit looking out at us instead of keeping their eyes on the road.

Quality Courts United, which began when seven southern motel owners split off from United Motor Courts in the late 1930s, issued some of the most distinctive brochure covers of the era. Seen here is a double-barreled color illustration of ideal motel life from the cover of a brochure first issued in the early 1940s.

Chapter 6

Motels and Motor Inns

ALL ROADS LEAD TO..

HAPPY HOLLOW

USA 70

HOTEL MOTEL

PARK

BATH HOUSE ROW

CENTRAL

ARMY NAVY HOSPITAL

230 FOUNTAIN STREET

HOT SPRINGS NATIONAL PARK ARKANSAS

Even the World War II era was a boom time for the motel industry, if not for so many other commercial establishments geared to the motoring public. Although many hostelries totally dependent upon the tourist trade went under, others thrived because of the national housing shortage and as temporary permanent housing near factories and military installations. But when the war was over, the rush was on to build newer and better facilities for the unfettered hordes once again able to pile on the miles.

The Holiday Motel in St. Petersburg, Florida, is a house of many gables.

Many veterans returning home decided to go into the lucrative motel business, opening small mom-and-pop operations along nearly every road. A manual funded by the Veterans' Administration in 1946 painted a rosy picture of the prospects for opening a roadside rest. But it also warned the faint of heart about the difficulties of running such a business: "The operation of a successful motor court takes hard work, 7 days a week, the year round. This endeavor should not be viewed as one where it is possible to sit in the sun by the side of the road and ring a cash register."

Nevertheless, the statistical data about the postwar motel boom is staggering. To cite one set of figures, there were some 20,000 motels in 1940, 30,000 in 1948, and 61,000 by 1960. By the late 1940s more than 86 percent of travelers were behind the wheels of their cars, and thus potential motel customers. By 1950 there were 22 million vacationers, and more than half of them stayed in motels. And by 1951 motels had surpassed hotels as the leading suppliers of rooms.

The architectural expression of these new businesses tended to be more practical

A room at the El Taoseno Court in Old Taos.

and mundane than the exuberant razzmatazz of the prewar years. Of course there was a carryover from the 1930s in the building of design wonders, thematic styles, and even latter-day interpretations of the snazzy Streamline Moderne. But for the most part the new buildings were small, nondescript interconnected lines of motel rooms with the registration office often an extension of the owner's home.

By today's standards, these motels of the 1940s and 1950s were still rather primitive affairs. In 1951 an average establishment had 25 rooms, but surprisingly, fewer than

It's common to see old Spanish theme motels, especially in New Mexico. The Buena Vista Pueblo on Highway 66 (top) is artistically rendered, silk-screen-like, on a postcard view. Food and drinks were "served in real southwestern style in the shade of adobe walls, while a Mexican orchestra provides the soft harmonious music of Old Spain." Unlike the Buena Vista, the La Casa Judy Motel in Santa Fe (above) makes only a slight curtsy to its Spanish heritage.

6 percent of all motels had pools; fewer than 8 percent had restaurants, even within walking distance; fewer than 20 percent had room phones; and fewer than 28 percent had any carpeting on the floors of the rooms. As in prewar auto courts, the motel of the 1950s still had virtually no interior public spaces. Yes, there would be a very small registration area, but there were few lobbies, lounges, and meeting rooms.

The evolution of the motel from a series of distinct cabins into continuous lines of rooms cannot be precisely documented, although the theory of evolution is quite clear. Interconnected lines of rooms were employed as early as 1929 at the Danish Village in Maine. In other places, especially in the 1930s, individual cabins were interconnected by roofs over parking places to protect the vehicles of each cabin's occupant.

At the English Motel on Highway 66 in Amarillo, Texas, the cabins were neoned Tudor in style and interconnected by covered garages.

Later on the garage spaces were walled in to provide additional rooms, and voilà, the continuous single-story motel had arrived. In other locations, such as the Dyer Cabins in Baldwin, Kansas, and at the Woahink Lake Court in Gardiner, Oregon, the garage space was incorporated within the shape of the cabin under a common roof, and the cabins, cheek-by-jowl, were linear, one-story structures.

Individual cabins were desirable for many reasons — they were or could be cute, attractive, and cozy, and they connoted a sense of privacy and individual "ownership" (if only for a night) in the same way that a freestanding house represents a concept of "home" more convincingly than an apartment or a connected townhouse. But cabins were also economically impractical as business operations. Each had to have separate heating, plumbing, and electrical connections. By joining rooms together, great economies in construction could be realized by the single, shared mechanical and electrical systems. And the maintenance of connected rooms and the surrounding landscape was easier and more efficient.

Instead of exhibiting individual architectural flair, the new interconnected motels looked pretty much the same. Differentiation was achieved by clever names, elaborate signs, and other cosmetic amenities. An excellent example of one such establishment was Don Lindgren's Westward Ho Motel. He decided to build a home on the range for tourists in 1953, and a discouraging word has seldom been heard for the past 40 years. Lindgren's range is on the plains of North

The Dyer Cabins in Baldwin, Kansas, catches individual cabins in the very act of turning into a continuous line of motel rooms: the garage has become part of the cabin form, and the cabins are attached.

By 1980 the Bayfield Wells Court in Bayfield, Colorado, was a bypassed relic. The scalloped cornice denotes the two rooms and their garages.

93

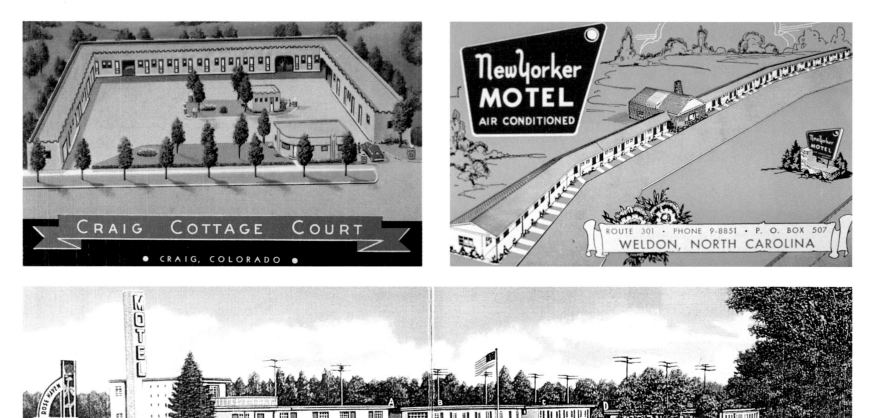

CRAIG COTTAGE COURT
• CRAIG, COLORADO •

NewYorker MOTEL AIR CONDITIONED
ROUTE 301 • PHONE 9-8851 • P. O. BOX 507
WELDON, NORTH CAROLINA

ROSE HAVEN MOTEL

Dakota, on the west side of Grand Forks, and the Westward Ho employs nearly every cowboy and western cliché in the book to establish its thematic identity.

The business began as a 40-room motel, and then, step by step, it grew into a tourist attraction. Now there are 108 motel rooms done up in western decor. There are meeting rooms, one seating up to 700 folks in a "convention center" masquerading as a frontier Main Street "Boot Hill"—type attraction; the Chuck House Ranch Restaurant serving

"fabulous breakfast vittles, chuck-wagon lunches, and grub steak dinners"; the Corral Gift Shop with a bevy of souvenirs; and even a Speakeasy Peanut Bar dedicated to that famous cowboy Al Capone.

All kiddin' aside, podner, this place is sophisticated commercial folk art, and tourists from miles around stop in to soak up the western atmosphere. To stop people passing by chance, the spacious grounds are embellished with 800 wagon wheels collected from all over North Dakota.

Single-story linear buildings were and are a popular and efficient design for motels. At the Craig Cottage Court a C-shaped configuration defines a common parking area. The New Yorker Motel bends only slightly as it just keeps rolling along beside Highway 301.

This double-panel linen postcard from 1950 of the Rose Haven in Gloucester City, New Jersey, is a grandiose statement of a humble building. The street sign, the perfectly placed lawn furniture, and even the lawn itself are admirable.

The Town House in Wichita Falls, Texas, was a motel on the move in the 1950s with TV, air conditioning, a restaurant next door, and a second-story wing at the rear.

The Riviera in Tucson, seen here in a tantalizing postcard view with room inset, was a motor hotel on the make. Already a second-story addition had been built—a quick way to double the number of rooms.

The institution of the motel, including the Westward Ho, made a quantum leap by the 1960s as it evolved into the motor inn or the motor hotel. These new accommodations were much more like the hotels that the original motor courts replaced, and they were much larger, often with 150 to 300 rooms. The rooms were in multistory buildings often arranged back-to-back along a central utility core. This was an efficient and economical way to build, but noisy for the guests who knew right away that another guest on the

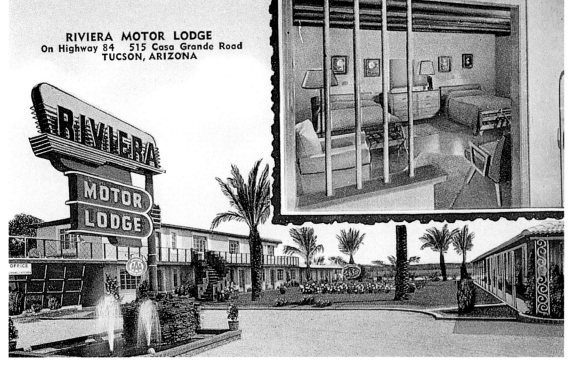

95

other side of the bathroom wall was taking a shower at five in the morning. Often the motor inns were located out by the new interstates — the very same highways that were a major factor in wiping out many of the smaller mom-and-pop operations of the past.

And these new motor inns were much more luxurious than their predecessors. Most had swimming pools in elaborately landscaped settings. There were bars, restaurants, coffee shops, meeting rooms, lobbies, and telephone switchboard service for the rooms—all of the comforts of a downtown hotel out on the edge of town. The domination of motels on the accommodations market was a fait accompli. In 1950 there were twice as many motels as hotels; by 1979 the ratio had climbed to four to one. Despite the growing sophistication of this new breed of motor hotels, they too would soon become an endangered species. The growing interstate highway system and the huge corporations that developed to service it began to replace the individually owned and operated establishments that had once superseded the old hotels.

A perfect family unit is about to check into a plastic motel room in this posed stock photo from about 1970.

The Le Mays Motel in Barre, Vermont, has a snug roadside presence with its 1950s curve-cornered roof and sheetrock siding.

That's the Sands of Tempe Motel seen just beyond and in front of the giant cheerleaders from adjacent Arizona State University, Tempe, in this postcard mailed in 1961. The evolution from a bunch of cabins was nearly complete. The "Sands" had an Olympic pool, a prime-rib restaurant, and convention facilities.

TRAIN MOTELS

Trains and motels have many common characteristics, not the least of which is the glamour and romance of travel itself. And so it shouldn't come as too big a surprise that there is a long tradition of using trains as places to house travelers. Many of the early train motels arose because of economic necessity—just using old trolley cars for something else. Other establishments played off of trains' distinctive identities. Cabooses, boxcars, and sleeping cars, permanently sided next to the road, have beckoned to tourists for most of the twentieth century.

The Sioux Chief Train Motel—four sleeping cars and a coach in Sioux Falls, South Dakota—was the inspiration of Verl Thomson, a campground owner with a big idea. This motel concept worked for a while in the 1960s and 1970s.

Four discarded railroad cars were used as tourist cabins in the 1930s in Lyons, Colorado. The rolling stock was once part of "the crack train of the C & S Railroad that ran to Leadville, Colorado."

The Motel 36 in Somerville, Texas—a railroad town—consisted of 11 boxcars, each converted into two 12 by 18-foot rooms. The "hobo motel," as it was nicknamed, had a centrally located caboose, right, which was used as a lounge for the boxcars. Brothers Hub and Eddie Baker thought up all of this in 1962.

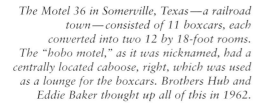

Donald M. Denlinger bought 19 cabooses as a motel and opened for business in 1970 in the tourist haven of Strasburg, Pennsylvania. Denlinger's children model the bunk beds available in a family unit. Now run by Kevin Cavanaugh, the business is chugging right along.

STREAMLINE AND DECO DELIGHTS

The Streamline Moderne and Art Deco were the very most up-to-date styles of the 1930s. Many motel owners seized upon the aura of this high style to create the most "modern" facilities for their clientele. This abstracted style of static objects seemingly in motion resulted in sinuous and snazzy motels, from the Shangri-La in Dodge City, Kansas, and the Palomar Motel in Shreveport, Louisiana, to the examples shown on these pages.

The Coral Court on Highway 66 just south of St. Louis, recently closed, is an intact, 1941 period piece. Most of the buildings contain two bedrooms connected centrally by two garages with foldout aluminum doors. The buildings are almost iridescent in their use of glass brick and gleaming glazed ceramic tile in a buff color with reddish brown accents. The Coral Court was placed on the National Register of Historic Places in 1989.

The Farmer Greene Motel office, Santa Claus, Georgia, was self-proclaimed as the latest and the greatest.

The Fountain Motel in Hot Springs, Arkansas, is a streamlined masterpiece dating from the late 1940s. And it's still there in all of its glory.

The Lynada Motel in Ogden, Utah, is seen here in a 1939 photograph used to produce a postcard. It had curvilinear awnings and round glass panes on the series of doors extending nearly to infinity. The 21 "fully carpeted" rooms were torn down about 1990.

THE MADONNA INN

I t's hard to miss the Madonna Inn, a huge complex of buildings beside Highway 101 in San Luis Obispo, California. It is a motel gone berserk—an enormous and ornate shrine to the vivid imagination, deep pockets, and compulsion for detail and perfection of Alex Madonna, a man who made his fortune in the road-building, construction, and cattle businesses.

The Madonna Inn began as a "normal" motel in the late 1950s, when a 12-room single-story structure was built. But work on the room interiors was delayed. That's when Alex and Phyllis Madonna took matters into their own hands and decided to make each room a distinctive thematic environment. By doing this Mr. and Mrs. Madonna hoped to cater to the different aesthetic inclinations of their potential customers. Working together the Madonnas

The main complex, completed in 1965, is a vast and rambling Swiss chalet–style building. Inside are the major public facilities —dining room, coffee shop, lobby, and gift shops.

Perhaps the most famous public place in the Madonna Inn is the men's room downstairs. A silent urinal becomes a waterfall when the electric eye mechanism is activated.

The Gold Rush Dining Room is a spectacle in itself. It is lighted by small bulbs hanging from the gold lighting fixtures made from leftover electrical conduit and scrap copper.

The coffee shop, with its carved wooden booths and murals, has copper-covered eating surfaces throughout. The special "Madonna pink" permeates everything everywhere. Below is a turkey sandwich from the coffee shop.

The Hilltop Unit, completed in a process that was part improvisation, is a two- to four-story building containing 84 fantastic bedrooms.

selected theme ideas and decor to fit each theme. In the early 1960s, two 14-room units were added on either side of the original building. Suddenly there were 40 stage-set motel rooms all in a row, and the wild and crazy Madonna Inn began to bloom.

The best rooms didn't come along until 1969, when the Hilltop Unit with 84 rooms was completed. But the extravagant Madonna style really reached fruition earlier with the building of the main complex in 1965. Using his expertise in highway construction and his own road crews, Alex Madonna designed and constructed this major building in a kind of Italian-Swiss style. It contains huge boulders, some on the exterior weighing up to 209 tons, with some interior fireplace stones weighing in at 15 tons.

The interior spaces of the main complex rival the most ornate public areas of the grand hotels of the early twentieth century. The Gold Rush Dining Room, seating up to 500 people, is decorated in bright "Madonna pink" with a custom-made floral carpet and a hand-carved marble balustrade. The entire room is romantically lit by small lightbulbs on the tendrils of an enormous gold tree fixture made from leftover electrical conduit and other remnants of copper. The 200-seat coffee shop has etched copper-covered counters and tabletops throughout. Sandwiches in the coffee shop are served on Madonna pink bread.

The Madonna Inn looked like an average little motel in the early 1960s, even though the rooms were already thematic in decor.

104

The Old Mill Room has a waterwheel and various cuckoo-clock-like gizmos built into the headboard of the bed.

But the most famous public room of all is the downstairs men's bathroom. It has a long, rock-lined urinal with an electric eye mechanism that causes a huge waterfall to descend as the lucky men eliminate. With other guests standing guard outside, women trespass to gawk at this grandiose wonder.

The state of the art in Madonna bedrooms is to be found in the 400-foot long, two- to four-story-high main guest-room building completed in 1969. Room themes, proudly proclaimed on hand-painted doors, are literal expressions developed with great imagination and originality. The cave-grotto rooms are probably the most popular, with walls and floors lined with rock panels. A four-foot crawl-space tunnel connects the Cave Man Room to the Daisy Mae, converting the two grottoes into a suite. The name of the Flintstone Room, which featured Fred Flintstone in leaded stained glass, had to be changed to Jungle Rock in the mid-1980s after Hanna-Barbera noted possible copyright infringement.

Cloud Nine, with its cónical ceiling and a suspended gold cherub above the bed, was made from an attic space.

The Austrian Suite, one of several devoted to various nationalities, is more than 70 feet long.

In addition to grottoes, there are rooms devoted to various nationalities, including several Swiss creations (the Madonnas have Swiss origins). There are round rooms, such as Ren, De, and Vous; a Buffalo Room, in which a former Madonna pet that met an unhappy end down by the highway has been stuffed, Trigger-like, and enshrined on the wall; and one irregular-shaped room, Tall and Short, with a bed five and one-half feet long on one side, six and one-half feet on the other.

The Madonna Inn is the grandest motel of them all, and it is the definitive expression of an individually owned and operated hostelry — light-years removed from the almost scientific sameness of the large franchised chains. It is a labor of love that became a labor of profit for the Madonnas — a place that needs to be experienced to be believed. To the intellectual cognoscenti it can be understood and dismissed or enjoyed as kitsch. To amazed visitors who've probably never even thought of "design" in formal terms, the Madonna Inn is a place full of joy, beauty, and one surprise after the next.

The hand-painted door to the Buffalo room proudly proclaims its theme. A Madonna pet that met an untimely end was stuffed and memorialized inside.

In the bathroom at the Old World Suite, the water for the sink descends from above in a diagonal trough.

FRANCHISE FIRSTS

Giant oaks from little acorns grow, someone once said. And so the motels pictured here speak of another time when today's lodging industry was in its infancy. In their own way these photographs are pivotal evidence of the very time when idiosyncracies were disappearing and standardization began to reign supreme.

Howard Johnson's began its motel career with nary an orange roof in sight. The first Hojo motel was of colonial red-brick design, and it opened in Savannah, Georgia, in 1954.

Merile K. Guertin ran the Beach Motel in Long Beach, California, when in 1947 he founded Best Western, now the world's largest chain of independently owned and operated motels.

The first Holiday Inn, which opened on the east side of Memphis, Tennessee, in 1952, was a prototype for many more to come.

The second unit in the Ramada Inn chain was this motel and pancake house in El Paso, Texas, seen here in 1962. The first Ramada was in Flagstaff, Arizona.

Scott King, who went on to found the TraveLodge chain after World War II, opened his first motel, the 15-cabin King's Auto Court, in San Diego, in 1935.

Chapter 7

Franchised Motels

"Somewhere in these states there is a young man who is going to become rich. He may be washing milk bottles in a dairy lunch. He is going to start a chain of small, clean, pleasant hotels, standardized and nationally advertised, along every important motor route in the country. He is not going to waste money on gilt and onyx, but he is going to have agreeable clerks, good coffee, endurable mattresses and good lighting; and in every hotel he will have at least one suite which, however small, will be as good as the average room in a great modern city hotel. He will invade every town which hasn't a good hotel already..." (Sinclair Lewis, *Saturday Evening Post,* January 3, 1920).

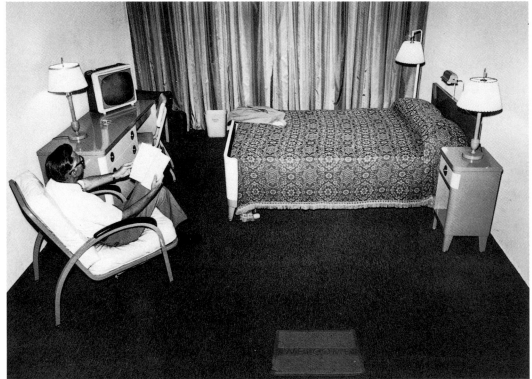

In 1951, Kemmons Wilson, a man in the home-building business in Memphis, hopped in his car and took a vacation trip to Washington, D.C., with his wife and five kids. As the Wilsons stayed in one motel after another along the way, Kemmons became increasingly depressed by the places they stayed in. He took notes, measured the rooms, and described this journey as "the most miserable vacation trip of my life." "As soon as I got back to Memphis," Wilson said, "I decided to build a motel that had all the things we missed." He wanted his motel to have a pool, a good restaurant, a gift shop, and for the kids to be able to stay free (he had been charged as much as two dollars a head to put up his kids during his vacation).

He handed his notes and measurements to Eddie Bluestein, a draftsman who worked for him, and three or four days later, Bluestein returned with a plan for a one-story motel. He had written the name "Holiday Inn" on top of the drawing because he had seen that very same Bing Crosby—Fred Astaire movie on TV the night before. Kemmons Wilson liked the plan and loved the name. He commissioned a local sign maker to build a 50-foot-high "great sign" (as they're called in the trade) modeled after a movie marquee (Mr. Wilson had owned and operated a popcorn stand in a Memphis movie theater when he was 17 years old). And in 1952, on the eastern edge of Memphis on the main drag, Sumner Avenue, he opened his first Holiday Inn with the

Holiday Inn was at the top of the hill as Kemmons Wilson was featured on the cover of Time *in 1972.*

The Holiday Inn room of the 1950s and 1960s was spartan and sturdy, but comfortable as well. This predictable certainty gave rise to the truth of the company's 1970s advertising slogan: "The best surprise is no surprise."

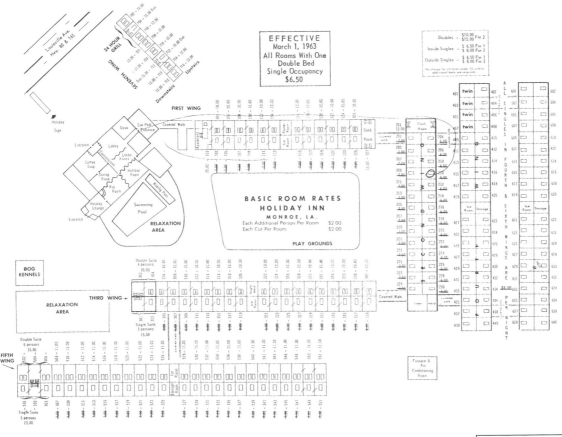

The floor plan of the two-story Holiday Inn was a standardized formula that worked equally well nearly everywhere in the late 1950s through the 1960s. It was economical to build, efficient to operate, and the prices at this Inn in Monroe, Louisiana, in 1963 were still friendly at $6.50 per night, single occupancy.

rooms decorated in chartreuse and white by his mother, Ruby "Doll" Wilson. The new Holiday Inn was the first major motel that travelers would pass as they came to Memphis from Nashville, and within a year, Wilson blanketed all of the major approaches to town by building three additional Inns to the north, south, and west. Wilson boasted to his wife that he wanted to build 400 motels, and little did he realize that would be just the beginning of the world's largest motel chain.

Collaborating with a Memphis associate, Wallace Johnson, president of the National Association of Home Builders, the pair decided to franchise their operation. They invited 68 builders to Memphis to sell the idea, and sell it they did. The first franchised

Holiday Inn opened in Clarksdale, Mississippi, in 1954, paying a fee of $500, plus a nickel per night per room to Wilson and Johnson's company. The first 75 Inns were one-story clones of the first one. But by the late 1950s the cheaper-to-build and larger two-story Holiday Inns became the rule.

From then on the Holiday Inn empire began an explosion of expansion. The 50th Inn was opened in Dyersburg, Tennessee, in 1958; the 100th in Tallahassee, Florida, in 1959; the 500th in Johnstown, Pennsylvania, in 1964; and the 1,000th in San Antonio, Texas, in 1968. When expansion was at its most intense, Kemmons Wilson estimated that a new Inn was being opened every three days and a new room was being built every 20 minutes.

Holiday Inns Inspection Department works constantly to insure you of Holiday Inn Standard service and accommodations.

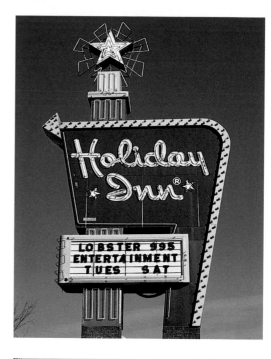

Holiday Inn stationery was cute and amiable in the 1960s. A series of drawings show John Holiday, an erstwhile Paul Revere-esque company symbol, and small vignettes of great moments in fun, relaxation, and business.

By the early 1960s a whole new generation of "budget" motels began to appear, with accommodations that undercut the price of facilities at the larger chains. The most famous and enduring of these outfits is Motel 6, founded by William Becker, a California painting contractor who went into partnership with a custom home builder and opened his first Motel 6 in Santa Barbara in 1962. Its rooms, stripped-down and smaller renditions of the larger chains' product, rented for $6 a night. They were up to $6.60 a night by the early 1970s. And today Motel 6, which describes itself as the largest chain of company-operated economy motels, has more than 750 outlets with rooms renting for the new inexpensive rate of about $25 a night. William Becker realized very early on that "motels almost put hotels out of business, but then the motels got fancy themselves. They beat the hotels and then turned around and joined them...."

Cecil Day, a devout Christian entrepreneur

from Atlanta, Georgia, was another important early player in the economy motel industry. Mr. Day decided that "no one was looking out for the middle American, the guy with two, three or four children travelling on a limited budget." He opened his first Days Inn of America in 1970, offering "luxury" budget rooms for $8 a night, and then began quickly to expand. Cecil Day tithed 10 percent of his profits to religious institutions and prided himself on using his motel business to give away a 700-page modern version of the Bible. On the book's yellow-and-black cover was inscribed "Take with you for Spiritual Uplift" (instead of the "Steal This Book" originally considered).

In the decade of the 1970s, the franchised motel business overwhelmed the market. While in 1970, 7 percent of the properties and 25 percent of the rooms were owned by chains, by 1978 nearly one-third of the properties and 70 percent of the rooms were chain-affiliated. In the past 30 years, as the

The changing of the guard in roadside design is clearly illustrated in the old and new Holiday Inn signs. The old sign (top), seen here as it stood in Ellsworth, Maine, was modeled after a movie marquee. The new sign (above), which replaced the original version in the 1980s—seen here in Brockton, Massachusetts—is tasteful and sedate because its role as a roadside lure had been supplanted by an 800 number and television advertising.

"formula" has been perfected, the facilities offered at one large chain have come to be barely distinguishable from those offered at another, except to the most experienced traveler. The vocabulary is universal, although the color of the carpet and drapes varies from room to room: size is about 13 by 20 feet; there are open-rack no-door closets with swipe-proof hangers; either a luggage rack or lots of flat space on low dressers, or both; a couple of beds and an armchair; tables, two table lamps, and a standing lamp; a TV set, a phone....

While the franchised motel room is a nearly perfect functional entity, it is nearly devoid of any "soul." And some observers, have condemned this new international style, among them the very eloquent architecture critic Ada Louise Huxtable, who wrote in a 1973 *New York Times* article entitled "Hospitality and the Plastic Esthetic": "And yet I never approach a trip requiring an overnight stay without a sinking heart. It's not that I won't be reasonably comfortable...it is that one is forced into a banal, standardized, multi-billion-dollar world of bad colors, bad fabrics, bad prints, bad pictures, bad furniture, bad lamps, bad ice-buckets and bad wastebaskets of such totally uniform and cheap consistency of taste and manufacture that borax or camp would be an exhilarating change of pace."

But not everyone is nearly as upset, sensitive, and aware as Ms. Huxtable. Most travelers accept the universal plastic room as an inevitable consequence of a group of large corporations all having attempted to solve

Albert Pick, a chain of hotels in 20 cities, was early to recognize the handwriting on the wall as the new motel chains were clobbering the old hotels in downtowns. By 1956, Albert Pick issued a most unhotel-like brochure announcing that it was operating six Holiday Inns in the South and Midwest.

Motel and hotel chains worked fervently to perfect their versions of the ideal room, standardized and formularized in every way. By 1973 in Southern California this process was so far along that one room was hard to distinguish from the next, except for the change in color of the carpet, drapes, and bedspreads. Shown here is the Hilton Inn Room, Laguna Hills, California.

the same problem. Most believe there is definitely something to be said in favor of the 1975 Holiday Inn advertising campaign that extolled the idea that "the best surprise is no surprise."

By the middle 1980s Holiday Inn abandoned and replaced its old green great sign with its distinctively articulated movie marquee shape and its splash of neon. It was superseded by a dark green inner-lit plastic sign with simple white letters spelling out "Holiday Inn" and a happy-face-like starburst design next to the name. This change in graphic style symbolized that the motel chains had almost obliterated the function of the "motel" that had given them their start. Now it no longer mattered very much what the building looked like, just as long as it was plain and unobtrusive; nor did the sign have to be designed to grab the attention of the passerby looking for a simple place to spend the night. The new expression of a chain hostelry is a sparse but direct graphic that is clearly discernable to those passing by at a high rate of speed on an interstate, and an array of national advertising tied into an 800 number for nearly instantaneous national

Ramada Inn, Beverly Hills, California.

Beverly Garland Howard Johnson's Motor Lodge, North Hollywood, California.

Holiday Inn, Santa Monica, California.

and international booking and reservations.

In today's mammoth hospitality industry the distinctions between a hotel room and a motel room have been blurred. Essentially they're the same commodity, sometimes offered up in a slightly different package. And the hotel-motels have expanded beyond the side of the road to build facilities at airports, in the heart of downtowns, and in resort settings. The American Hotel and Motel Association, which keeps tabs on the industry, doesn't bother to distinguish between the two as it compiles its tabs of statistics about the state of the world of sleep.

Although many brand names of the large motel chains from the 1950s and 1960s have survived, now many of these names share a common ownership. And nearly none of the original owners are around anymore. Kemmons Wilson sold Holiday Inn in 1990 to a British conglomerate, Bass (as in Bass Ale) PLC, and there are now some 1,800 Holiday Inns with 340,000 rooms worldwide. Saturation of the market is nearly complete: by 1988 some 96 percent of American motel users had stayed in a Holiday Inn.

117

Quality Courts, which became Quality Inns, is part of Choice Hotels International, which claims to have introduced the concept of "brand segmentation" to the hotel industry: limited-service budget hotels (many of these are motels), mid-priced full-service, and full-service luxury. Worldwide, Choice Hotels franchises some 3,000 hotels with 271,000 rooms under such names as Quality, Comfort, Choice, Sleep, Econolodge, Rodeway, and Friendship. An outfit called Hospitality Franchise Systems runs some 2,500 hotels with 300,000 rooms under the brand names of Howard Johnson's, Ramada Inn, Days Inn, and Super 8.

The motel, an idea made necessary and indispensable at the beginning of the twentieth century, has in its history been called a myriad of terms—camps, cabins, and courts being among the most common. The word "motel" itself has now become obsolete. It sounds too funky and old-fashioned; its time has come and gone. Now, in the era of mega-corporations and gigantic chains, motels are called inns, hotels, lodges, or suites—anything but motels.

Across the United States, especially in smaller places bypassed by the fast lanes of

TraveLodge's Sleepy Bear symbol, shown here in a die-cut double postcard souvenir, is the friendliest and fuzziest corporate symbol in the contemporary lodging industry. It was adopted by the company in 1954, partially in homage to the Golden Bear symbol of California. Unlike the Golden Bear, somnambulistic Sleepy wears a long-sleeved night-shirt and nightcap emblazoned with his name.

the interstates and by "civilization" as we now know it, there are still family owned and operated motels of great distinction. They offer peace and quiet, comfortable and immaculate rooms, hard beds and very good restaurants, and they are often bargains when compared to the prices of the big chains. But like any other product of individuality and excellence, they are getting harder and harder to find.

Many of the old motels have gotten as old as the "moms" and "pops" who started them, and they will eventually fade away. But in the decline of these family owned businesses beside the road there is the loss of a certain personal touch, a little bit of individuality—a family pet wandering around the premises, a well-kept flower garden, a hominess that is lacking in the places that have everything all figured out. Some of these motels market themselves as a pleasant and economical alternative to the mold. Camps, cabins, courts, and motels, lodging types that span the entire history of the genre, are still available to the adventuresome tourist. The most fabulous old motels of them all, however, are the ones that aren't there anymore — victims of progress and sophistication.

Howard Johnson's, soon after opening its first motel in Savannah in 1954—in a building that looked more like a red-brick high school or city hall than a motel—began to use an orange roof as a way for motorists to identify its lodgings. For nearly 20 years the chain built orange-roofed "Gate Lodge" motor lobbies, as seen here in a 1958 magazine advertisement; an orange-roofed Hojo restaurant was right next door.

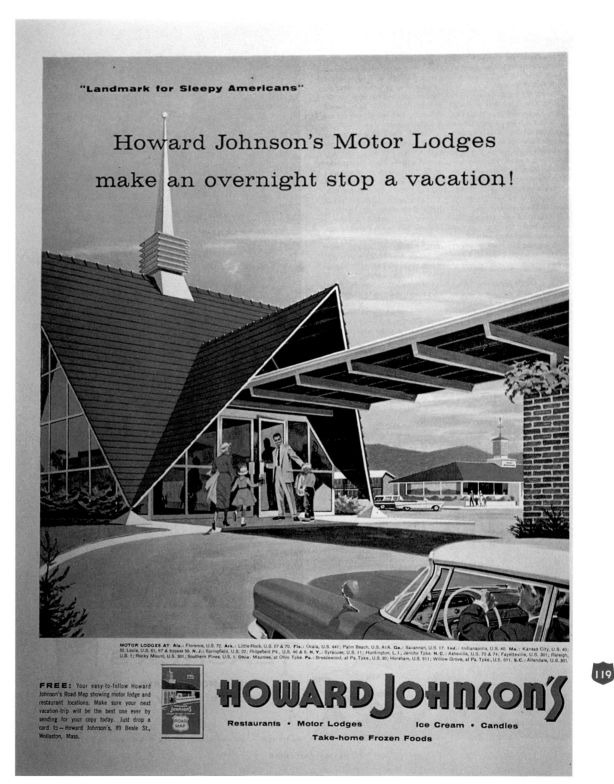

"Landmark for Sleepy Americans"

Howard Johnson's Motor Lodges
make an overnight stop a vacation!

MOTOR LODGES AT Ala.: Florence, U.S. 72. Ark.: Little Rock, U.S. 67 & 70. Fla.: Ocala, U.S. 441; Palm Beach, U.S. A1A. Ga.: Savannah, U.S. 17. Ind.: Indianapolis, U.S. 40. Mo.: Kansas City, U.S. 40; St. Louis, U.S. 61, 67 & bypass 50. N. J.: Springfield, U.S. 22; Ridgefield Pk., U.S. 46 & 6. N. Y.: Syracuse, U.S. 11; Huntington, L. I., Jericho Tpke. N. C.: Asheville, U.S. 70 & 74; Fayetteville, U.S. 301; Raleigh, U.S. 1; Rocky Mount, U.S. 301; Southern Pines, U.S. 1. Ohio: Maumee, at Ohio Tpke. Pa.: Breszewood, at Pa. Tpke., U.S. 30; Horsham, U.S. 611; Willow Grove, at Pa. Tpke., U.S. 611. S.C.: Allendale, U.S. 301.

FREE: Your easy-to-follow Howard Johnson's Road Map showing motor lodge and restaurant locations. Make sure your next vacation-trip will be the best one ever by sending for your copy today. Just drop a card to—Howard Johnson's, 89 Beale St., Wollaston, Mass.

HOWARD JOHNSON'S

Restaurants • Motor Lodges   Ice Cream • Candies
Take-home Frozen Foods

119

MOTEL MEMORIES

Old motels not only go out of business, they often suffer the indignity of abandonment as well. It isn't that easy to find a new use for an old motel. Yes, some have become housing for the elderly and for students. Others became flea markets. Abandoned motels are compelling icons as they submit to the forces of decay. They are the ghosts of small businesses, having outlived the moms and pops who built them.

On Route 9, Cold Spring, New York, 1978.

Wiley's Resort Motel, Highway 40, Dinosaur, Colorado, 1991.

Near Nickel Creek, Texas, 1993.

ACKNOWLEDGMENTS

THANKS TO: Those people who helped to bring this book into being: Terry Hackford, editor and guiding light; Eric Baker and Mathieu Araud, book designers extraordinaire; Tom Todd for his excellent slides of flat materials; Kevin C. Downs for his beautiful large-format color transparencies; Mark DelFranco and Ezra Ernst for their expert advice; and David Coen, eagle-eyed copy editor.

Those people who were especially helpful and generous in the sharing of their time, knowledge, and visual resources: Vetra Long for her faithful correspondence, evocative memories, and artifacts from the Wigwam Village motel chain; Roger B. White at the Division of Transportation, National Museum of American History, for his knowledge and insights, and for providing access to the department's extensive files about motel matters; and David L. Cole for making available his splendid collection of motelabilia and research.

Those organizations and individuals who helped to sponsor and underwrite the cost of the photography: The Architectural League of New York; Tom Bailey; Asher Edelman; Rosalie Genevro; the Howard Gilman Foundation; Toni Greenberg; the John Simon Guggenheim Memorial Foundation; Agnes Gund; Ellen Harris; Barbara Jakobson; Philip Johnson; Rick Landau; the Sidney and Francis Lewis Foundation; Jim McClure; the Design Arts and the Visual Arts Programs of the National Endowment for the Arts in Washington, D.C., a federal agency; the New York Foundation for the Arts; Susan Plum; Harold Ramis; and Virginia Wright.

Those individuals and organizations who gave access to their private collections, and those who gave of their time, knowledge, and resources in the preparation of this book: Billy Adler; Lew Baer; Bill Barry at the Maine Historical Society; Joan Blatterman; Ralph Bowman; Susan Box at the Phillips Petroleum Company; Shirley E. Braunlich at the Lawrence (Kans.) Public Library; Ron Brister at the Memphis (Tenn.) Museum System; Andreas Brown at the Gotham Book Mart, New York City; Brian Butko; Amy Canadee, Ritter Public Library, Vermilion, Ohio; Joanne Cassullo; Kevin Cavanaugh at the Red Caboose Motel, Strasburg, Pa.; Inez E. Cline, Hysterical Historian, Hot Springs, Ark.; Eleanor Caldwell; Betsy Cromley; Bob Davis and Jackie Gray at the Motel Inn; John and Jean Dunning; Tara Edwards; David Farmer and Kay Bost at the DeGolyer Library, Southern Methodist University; David Gebhard; Henry Golas at Tomesha Corp.; Debra Gust at the Curt Teich Postcard Archives; Jim Heimann; Kevin Holloway at the American Petroleum Institute Library; Steve Jansen at the Watkins Community Museum, Lawrence, Kans.; Mary C. Keane at the Mobil Corporation; Ken Kneitel; Carolyn Kozo-Cole at the Security Pacific Collection, Los Angeles Public Library; Cynthia R. Krimmel at the San Diego Historical Society; Bob and Mary Kurey; Gary F. Kurutz at the California State Library Photography Collection; Kevin Kutz; Patricia LaPointe at the Memphis (Tenn.)

and Shelby County Public Library; Al Lathrop at the Northwest Architectural Archives, St. Paul, Minn.; Don Lindgren at the Westward Ho Motel, Grand Forks, N.Dak.; Alex and Phyllis Madonna; Ginny Mahoney; Randell L. Makinson at the Greene and Greene Library, Pasadena, Calif.; Jim Masson; Bonnie McClintook at the Morris County Historical Society, Council Grove, Kans.; Thomas O. Muldoon; Paul W. Muller; Rich Musante; Bruce Nelson; Mary Newman; Kirk Oehlerking at the Log Cabin Inn Motel, Eureka Springs, Ark.; Hal Ottaway; Leland and Crystal Payton; Karl Perry at the Forest Service/USDA; Christina Petoski; Don and Newly Preziosi; Catherine Renschler at the Adams County Historical Society, Hastings, Nebr.; Paula Rubenstein; Beth L. Savage at the National Register of Historic Places; Elliot Sherman; Natalie Shivers; Betty N. Soper at the Platte County (Mo.) Historical Society; Karen Shatzkin; Marcella Stark of the Foudren Library, Southern Methodist University; David Streeter of the Pomona (Calif.) Public Library; Roger Steckler; Jane Stubbs; Van Summerill; Kathie Tietze; Michael and Marion Usher; Joseph Vasta; John and Patti Vierra; Fred and Barb Volkman; Gary Witt; Mrs. Robert E. Woods at the Exelsior Springs (Mo.) Historical Museum; and Tom Zimmerman.

The helpful and friendly people in the lodging industry who assisted with the research and contributed visual materials: Omar E. Akchurin, Daille G. Pettit, and Laura Turbe at the American Hotel and Motel Association; Skip Boyer, Patty Nowack, and Nancy Vaughn at Best Western International; Ann Curtis and Maggie Shubert at Choice Hotels International; Robert E. Bibeault at Hilton Inns; Craig Smith and Carrie Whiteman at Holiday Inn Worldwide; Lisa Garb of Howard Johnson Franchise Systems; Mary Boyce at ITT Sheraton Corporation; Marc Michaelson of Motel 6; Liz Elman of Ramada Franchise Systems; and Alexandra Kent and Brenda Shields at Forte Hotels.

SOURCE CREDITS

All contemporary color photographs, unless otherwise noted, were taken by John Margolies in the years noted in the source list below or in the text illustration caption. Additional contemporary color photographs as follows: *page 102* (bottom) courtesy the Madonna Inn; *pages 103–107* color photographs by TELETHON (Billy Adler and John Margolies), 1972; *pages 116–117* color photographs by TELETHON (Billy Adler and John Margolies), 1973.

All supplementary visual material is from the author's collection, except as noted.

Endleaves Symbols and logos for auto camps, cabin courts, and motels, 1920s through 1950s: California Camp Owners Association, Jim Masson Collection; The Approved Wayside Stations, Inc., David L. Cole Collection; American Tourist Camp Association, DeGolyer Library Collection, Southern Methodist University, Dallas, Texas.

Page 1 Line art from matchbook cover, courtesy of the Resthaven Motel, Santa Monica, California.

Page 2 Pilgrim Court, Washington, Mississippi, 1986.

Page 3 Stock cut for matchbook cover, Match Corporation of America, c. 1950.

Pages 4–5 Matchbook cover for R. Mars, The Contract Company, Washington, D.C.

Page 6 (top) White border postcard, Don and Newly Preziosi Collection; (bottom) postcard, c. 1910.

Page 7 UPI/Bettmann.

Pages 8–9 (top) *Fortune*, September 1934, pp. 54–55.

Page 9 (bottom) Line drawing from South of the Border Motel brochure, Dillon, South Carolina, c. 1960.

Page 10 (left) 1982; (right) 1993.

Page 11 (clockwise from top left): 1988; (Siesta Motel) 1991; 1980; 1980; 1984.

Page 12 (clockwise from top left): 1991; 1988; 1988.

Page 13 (clockwise from top left): 1984; (Rocket Motel) 1979; 1982; 1980; 1984.

Page 14 Detail from Ruckstell Axle magazine advertisement, *Motor Camper & Tourist*, May 1925, back cover.

Page 15 Used with permission of Parker Brothers. All rights reserved.

Page 16 (left) Advertising card, c. 1925; (right) brochure cover, c. 1925, David L. Cole Collection.

Page 17 (right) Security Pacific Collection/Los Angeles Public Library.

Page 18 Gotham Book Mart, New York City.

Page 19 (top) USDA Forest Service, F. E. Colburn, photographer; (bottom) advertising blotter, c. 1930.

Page 20 (both) California State Library, Sacramento, California.

Page 21 (top) White border postcard, c. 1920s, Don and Newly Preziosi Collection; (bottom) white border postcard, Haynes Photo, c. 1920s,

Gotham Book Mart, New York City.

Page 23 (top) Real-photo postcard, Bruce Nelson Collection; (bottom) line drawing detail from back cover of Camp New York brochure, c. 1925, David L. Cole Collection.

Page 24 (clockwise from left): Dexter Press photograph; Bruce Nelson Collection; Zagelmeyer Auto Camp Company brochure, Bay City, Michigan, 1928.

Page 25 (top) USDA Forest Service; (bottom) line drawing detail from magazine advertisement for Prairie-Schooner Trailer Company, Elkhart, Indiana, *Automobile and Travel Trailer Magazine,* September 1941, p. 27.

Page 26 Line drawing detail from business card for Sagamore Rest, Sagamore, Massachusetts, c. 1950s.

Page 27 1984.

Page 28 (top) Postcard postmarked 10/2/15, Hal Ottaway Collection; (bottom) Elliot Sherman Collection.

Page 29 (clockwise from left) Real-photo postcard, c. 1920s, Gotham Book Mart, New York City; Dexter Press photo, c. 1930s.

Page 30 (bottom) Linen postcard, c. 1930s.

Pages 30–31 (top) DeGolyer Library Collection, Southern Methodist University, Dallas, Texas, F. Morrison Boyd, photographer.

Page 32 (top) Two-panel linen postcard; (bottom) real-photo postcard, Hal Ottaway Collection.

Page 33 (clockwise from upper left) 1982; Dexter Press photo, c. 1930s; Archive Photos.

Page 34 (clockwise from top left) 1980; 1980; Dexter Press photo, c. 1940.

Page 35 1977.

Page 36 1980.

Page 37 (top) 1984; (bottom) 1994.

Page 38 (both) Maine Historical Society.

Page 39 (bottom) Courtesy of the Library of Congress.

Page 40 Real-photo postcard.

Page 41 (top) Dexter Press photo, Edward D. Hipple, photographer; (bottom) windshield sticker.

Page 42 (top) 1991; (bottom) real-photo postcard,

John Dunning Collection.

Page 43 (clockwise from top left) 1988; Dexter Press photo; 1985; real-photo postcard.

Pages 44–45 Courtesy of the Dohanos family heirs.

Page 46 Division of Transportation, National Museum of American History, 5/21/50, and courtesy of Tribune Media Services.

Page 47 (left) Chrome postcard, Don and Newly Preziosi Collection; (right) 1991.

Page 48 1991.

Page 49 Tom Zimmerman Collection.

Page 50 (top) White border postcard, Gotham Book Mart, New York City; (bottom) floor plan from Utah Motor Court brochure, 1932, David L. Cole Collection.

Page 51 (top) Linen postcard; (bottom) real-photo postcard.

Page 52 (clockwise from top) 1984; 1984; 1980.

Page 53 (clockwise from top left) Dexter Press photo; linen postcard, Don and Newly Preziosi Collection; 1987.

Page 54 (left) Courtesy of Choice Hotels International.

Page 55 (clockwise from top left) 1987; chrome postcard, Don and Newly Preziosi Collection; chrome postcard.

Page 56 (top) Real-photo postcard; (bottom) matchbook cover, c. 1930s, courtesy of Phillips Petroleum Company.

Page 57 (clockwise from top) Linen postcard; line drawing from Holiday Inn Room Service Menu, c. 1960, courtesy of Holiday Inn Worldwide; real-photo postcard.

Page 58 (bottom) Real-photo postcard postmarked 1/7/39, Hal Ottaway Collection.

Page 59 (clockwise from top left) Linen postcard, Gotham Book Mart, New York City; 1974; Dexter Press photo.

Page 60 Linen postcards.

Page 61 (clockwise from top) Linen postcard, Gotham Book Mart, New York City; 1978; Dexter Press photo.

Page 62 (clockwise from top) White border postcard postmarked 1936; real-photo postcard; Gordon L. Hickson, photographer.

Page 63 (both) 1987.

Page 64 (clockwise from top left) Linen postcard; in-room tent card, courtesy of Best Western International; Gotham Book Mart, New York City.

Page 65 (clockwise from top left) 1982; 1990; FPG International.

Page 66 Two-panel postcard distributed by the Mainliner Motel, Beloit, Kansas. Courtesy of Best Western International.

Page 68 (top) The Heineman Collection, The Greene and Greene Library, The Gamble House, University of Southern California, Pasadena, California; 1976.

Page 69 (top to bottom) Linen postcard; magazine advertising illustrations, *Wayside Salesman,* March 1931.

Page 71 (both) 1979.

Page 72 (left and right) Paula Rubenstein Collection, 1931; (center) courtesy of Proctor & Gamble.

Page 73 Brochure illustration, 1959, courtesy of Choice Hotels International.

Page 74 (top) Chrome postcard; (bottom) linen postcard, both from the Don and Newly Preziosi Collection.

Page 75 (lower right) 1993.

Page 76 (left) 1987; (right) white border postcard postmarked 3/1/30.

Page 77 (clockwise from top) Linen postcard, Don and Newly Preziosi Collection; 1980; 1991.

Page 78 (center) Uniform patch, Vetra Long Collection; (right) 1979, Cave City, Kentucky.

Page 79 (top) Don and Newly Preziosi Collection; (bottom) linen postcard, 1948.

Page 80 (top) 1977; (bottom) Vetra Long Collection.

Page 81 (left) Vetra Long Collection; (right) linen postcards.

Page 82 (left) 1979.

Pages 82–83 1977.

Page 83 (clockwise from upper right) Real-photo postcard by Studio Beauchamp, St. Eustache, P.Q.;

linen postcard, Don and Newly Preziosi Collection; UPI/Bettmann, 4/28/36.

Page 84 Paula Rubenstein Collection.

Page 86 (left) Jim Masson Collection; (top center and right) David L. Cole Collection.

Page 87 Courtesy of Choice Hotels International.

Page 88 Linen postcard back.

Page 89 1980.

Page 90 1980.

Page 91 (clockwise from top left) Postcard detail, and right, postcard, both Hal Ottaway Collection; 1979.

Page 92 1982.

Page 93 (both) 1980.

Page 94 (clockwise from top left) Linen postcard; chrome postcard; two-panel linen postcard.

Page 95 (top) Linen postcard; (bottom) chrome postcard.

Page 96 Archive Photos.

Page 97 (top) 1984; (bottom) chrome postcard postmarked 6/22/61, Don and Newly Preziosi Collection.

Page 98 (top) 1980; (bottom) UPI/Bettmann.

Page 99 (clockwise from top left) 1982; Wide World Photo; 1989; Red Caboose Motel, Strasburg, Pennsylvania.

Page 100 (all) 1988.

Page 101 (from top) Dexter Press photo; 1980; Dexter Press photo.

Pages 102–103 Line drawing courtesy of the Madonna Inn.

Page 104 (bottom) Courtesy of the Madonna Inn.

Page 108 (top) Courtesy of Howard Johnson Franchise Systems; (bottom) courtesy of Holiday Inn Worldwide.

Pages 108–109 Courtesy of Best Western International.

Page 109 (top) Courtesy of Ramada Franchise Systems, Inc.; (bottom) San Diego Historical Society Photograph Collection.

Page 110 Holiday Inn logo from 1956 Holiday Inn Directory, Brian Butko Collection, courtesy of Holiday Inn Worldwide.

Page 111 Courtesy of Holiday Inn Worldwide.

Page 112 (left) Time Inc., reprinted by permission;

(right) Division of Transportation, National Museum of American History, courtesy of Holiday Inn Worldwide.

Page 113 (top) Motel guest map, Holiday Inn, c. 1960, courtesy of Holiday Inn Worldwide; (bottom) line art from Holiday Inns of America Directory, Fall & Winter 1964, p. 41, courtesy of Holiday Inn Worldwide.

Page 114 (clockwise from left) Courtesy of Holiday Inn Worldwide; 1985; 1985.

Page 115 Brian Butko Collection, courtesy of Holiday Inn Worldwide.

Page 116 Courtesy of Hilton Hotels Corporation and Ramada Franchise Systems, Inc.

Page 117 Courtesy of Howard Johnson Franchise Systems and Holiday Inn Worldwide.

Page 118 Courtesy of Forte Hotels, Inc.

Page 119 Courtesy of Howard Johnson Franchise Systems.

Page 122 Los Angeles, California, 1973.

Page 123 Die-cut two-panel postcard.

Page 125 Busy person's correspondence postcard, Brian Butko Collection.

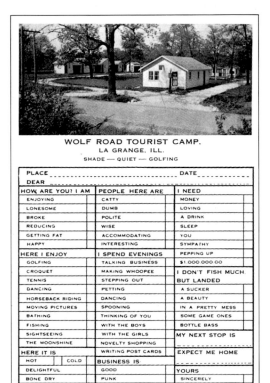

Page 127 Stock cuts for matchbook covers, Match Corporation of America, c. 1950

Page 128 Monroeville, Ohio, 1980.

BIBLIOGRAPHY

BOOKS

Anderson, Warren H. *Vanishing Roadside America*. University of Arizona Press, 1981.

Anderson, Will. *Mid-Atlantic Roadside Delights*. Anderson & Sons' Publishing Company, 1991.
———. *New England Roadside Delights*. Will Anderson Publisher, 1989.

Andrews. J.J.C. *The Well-Built Elephant and Other Roadside Attractions: A Tribute to American Eccentricity*. Congdon & Weed, 1984.

Ansaldi, Richard. *Souvenirs from the Roadside West*. Harmony Books, 1978.

Ant Farm. *Automerica: A Trip Down U.S. Highways from World War II to the Future*. E. P. Dutton & Company, 1976.

Automobile Club of America. *Tour Book*. Automobile Club of America, 1911.
Baeder, John. *Gas, Food and Lodging*. Abbeville Press, 1982.

Baker, Eric, and Tyler Blik. *Trademarks of the 20's and 30's*. Chronicle Books, 1986.
———. *Trademarks of the 40's and 50's*. Chronicle Books, 1988.

Baker, Eric, and Jane Martin. *Great Inventions, Good Intentions: An Illustrated History of Design Patents*. Chronicle Books, 1990.

Baker, Geoffrey, and Bruno Funaro. *Motels*. Reinhold Publishing Corporation, 1955.

Belasco, Warren James. *Americans on the Road: From Autocamp to Motel, 1910–1945*. The MIT Press, 1979.

Blake, Peter. *God's Own Junkyard: The Planned*

Brener, Sephen W. *The Motor Hotel Becomes of Age.* Reprint from Appraisal and Valuation Manual, American Society of Appraisers, 1962, pp. 81–92.

Brent, William and Milarde. *Grand Motel.* Greenberg: Publisher, 1955.

Denlinger, Donald M. *Red Caboose Motel: How It All Started.* Stel-Mar, n.d. (c. 1980).

Edwards, Jim, and Hal Ottaway. *The Vanished Splendor II: A Postcard Album of Oklahoma City.* Abalache Book Shop Publishing Company, 1983.

Gebhard, David. *Robert Stacy-Judd: Maya Archictecture, the Creation of a New Style.* Capra Press, 1993.

Gebhard, David, and Harriette Von Breton. *Los Angeles in the Thirties: 1931–1941.* 1975. Second Edition, Revised and Enlarged. Hennessey & Ingalls, 1989.

Gruber, J. Richard. *Memphis—1948–58.* Exhibition Catalog, Memphis Brooks Museum of Art, 1986. "Sumner Avenue: Roadside Archictecture and the Evolution of the American Motel," pp. 118–127; "Interview…Kemmons Wilson," pp. 128–133.

Harding, R. Brewster. *Roadside New England 1900–1955: A Photographic Postcard Record of the Eastern Illustrating & Publishing Company of Belfast, Maine.* Old Port Publishing Company, 1982.

Heimann, Jim, and Rip Georges. *California Crazy: Roadside Vernacular Architecture.* Chronicle Books, 1980.

(Heineman, Arthur S.) *Milestone Mo-Tels: Motor Hotels* (prospectus). Milestone Interstate Corporation, 1925.

Hilton, Conrad. *Be My Guest.* Prentice Hall Press, 1957.

Hine, Thomas. *Populuxe.* Alfred A. Knopf, 1986.

Hines, Duncan. *Adventures in Good Eating.* Duncan Hines, 1950.
——. *Lodging for a Night.* Duncan Hines, 1947.

Hokanson, Drake. *The Lincoln Highway: Main Street Across America.* University of Iowa Press, 1988.

Jackson, John Brinckerhoff. *Discovering the Vernacular Landscape.* Yale University Press, 1984.

Jackson, J. B. *Landscapes.* University of Massachusets Press, 1970.
——. *The Necessity for Ruins and Other Topics.* University of Massachusetts Press, 1980.

Jakle, John A. *The Tourist: Travel in Twentieth-Century North America.* University of Nebraska Press, 1985.

Jennings, Jan, ed. *Roadside America: The Automobile in Design and Culture.* Iowa State University Press for the Society for Commercial Archeology, 1990. "The Motel in Builder's Literature and Architectural Publications: An Analysis of Design," by Mary Ann Beecher, pp. 115–124; "Frank Redford's Wigwam Village Chain: A Link in the Modernization of the American Roadside," by Keith A. Sculle, pp. 125–135.

Johnson, Wallace E., with Eldon Roark. *Work Is My Play.* Hawthorn Books, 1973.

Kashiwabara, Yosh. *Matchbook Art.* Chronicle Books, 1990.

Kelly, Susan Croce. Photographic Essay by Quinta Scott. *Route 66.* University of Oklahoma Press, 1988.

Liebs, Chester H. *Main Street to Miracle Mile: American Roadside Architecture.* New York Graphic Society/Little, Brown & Company, 1985.

Long, John D., and J. C. Long. *Motor Camping.* Revised Edition. Dodd, Mead and Company, 1926.

Love, Harry Barclay. *Establishing and Operating a Year-Round Motor Court.* Office of Small Business, U.S. Department of Commerce, 1946.

Luxenburg, Stan. *Roadside Empires: How the Chains Franchised America.* Viking Penguin, Inc., 1985.

Margolies, John. *The End of the Road: Vanishing Highway Architecture in America.* Penguin Books in Collaboration with the Hudson River Museum, 1977, 1978, 1981.
——. *Pump and Circumstance: Glory Days of the Gas Station.* Bulfinch Press/Little, Brown & Company, 1993.

Margolies, John, and Emily Gwathmey. *Signs of Our Time.* Abbeville Press, 1993.

Marling, Karal Ann. *The Colossus of Roads: Myth and Symbol along the American Highway.* University of Minnesota Press, 1984.

Nabokov, Vladimir. *Lolita.* Reprint. Vintage Internatinal, 1989.

Partridge, Bellamy. *Fill'er Up!: The Story of Fifty Years of Motoring.* McGraw-Hill, 1952.

Patton, Phil. *Open Road: A Celebration of the American Highway.* Simon & Schuster, 1986.

Retskin, Bill. *The Matchcover Collector's Price Guide.* WorldComm, 1993.

Roberts, Kenneth L. *Sun Hunting.* The Bobbs-Merrill Company, 1922.

Schlereth, Thomas J. *US 40: A Roadscape of the American Experience.* Indiana Historical Society, 1985.

Sears, Stephen W. *The American Heritage History of the Automobile in America.* American Heritage Publishing Company, 1977.

Steele, Thomas, Jim Heimann, and Rod Dyer. *Close Cover Before Striking: The Golden Age of Matchbook Art.* Abbeville Press, 1987.

Steinbeck, John. *Travels With Charley: In Search of America.* Reprint. Penguin Books, 1986.

Venturi, Robert, Denise Scott Brown, and Steven Izenour. *Learning from Las Vegas.* 1977. Revised Edition. MIT Press, 1972.

Wallis, Allan D. *Wheel Estate: The Rise and Decline of Mobile Homes.* Oxford University Press, 1991.

Wallis, Michael. *Route 66: The Mother Road.* St. Martin's Press, 1990.

(Webb, Del E.) *Del E. Webb Motor Hotels* (promotional book). Del E. Webb Motor Hotel Co., n.d. (c. 1958).

(White, Roger B.) *At Home on the Road* (exhibition brochure). Division of Transportation, National Museum of American History, November 15, 1985, to January 1987.

White, Stewart Edward. *Camp and Trail.* Doubleday, Page & Company, 1915.

Wilson, Kemmons. *The Holiday Inn Story* (promotional booklet). Second Edition. Holiday Inns, Inc., 1972.

Wright, Warren. *"…by my own mind and hands…"* (biography of Bill Farmer in Alamo Plaza Motel chain). Quality Printing Co., 1975.

Young & Rubicam, Inc. *Roadside Housing Survey*, March 1948.

PERIODICALS

American Heritage. "The Great American Motel," by Paul Lancaster, June/July 1982, pp. 100–108.

The American Magazine. "Camps of Crime," by J. Edgar Hoover with Courtney Ryley Cooper, February 1940, pp. 14–15 and 130–132.

American Motorist. "All Aboard for Open Roads and a Care-Free Gypsy Life!," by John Anson Ford, April 1921, pp. 5–9.
——. "Driveway in New Denver Camp Deeded to Nation's Motorists"(Overland Park), by Warren E. Boyer, October 1922, pp. 6–7 and 30.
——. "Cincinnati's Free Motor Tourist Park," by J. J. Pfiester, November 1922, pp. 19 and 30.

Best Western Compass Magazine. "50 Years of Moving On," by William H. Skip Boyer, vol. 2, no. 3, pp. 2–7.

Bulb Horn. "An Unforgettable 1927 Journey in a Model T Ford," by Ross Zimmerman, January–March 1988, pp. 26–27.
——. "California or Bust in 1924," by Ray Heit, April–June 1988, pp. 35–37.

Business Week. "America Takes to the Motor Court," June 15, 1940, pp. 20–22.

Car Collector. "Sinclair Lewis, Gasoline Gypsy," by Albert D. Manchester, March 1989, pp. 54–55.

Cornell H.R.A. Quarterly. "Hospitality History: Who Wrote What About When," by Robert H. Woods, August 1991, pp. 89–94.

The Daily Standard (Excelsior Springs, Mo.). "Privacy and Comfort of Modern Home to Be Found in Model Tourist City," May 20, 1931.
——. "Formal Opening of Model Tourist City Set for Saturday and Sunday," July 7, 1931, p. 1.
——. "Formal Opening of Tourist City on for Weekend," July 10, 1931.

Esquire. "Grand Motel," by Billy Adler and John Margolies, July 1976, pp. 98–101.

Fortune. "The Great American Roadside," unsigned (by James Agee), paintings by John Steuart Curry, September 1934, pp. 53–63, 172, 174, and 177.
——. "Money on the Roadside," August 1951

Greater Portland. "Maine's Danish Village," by Bill Barry and Debra Verrier, vol. 27, no. 3, Fall 1982, pp. 50–55.

Hospitality. "A Thumbnail Guide to Chains," December 1972, pp. 34–44.

Journal of Cultural Geography. "Motel by the Roadside: America's Room for the Night," by John A. Jakle, Fall–Winter 1980, pp. 34–49.

Kansas Historical Quarterly. "The Municipal Campgrounds of Kansas," by Clinton Warne, vol. 29, no. 2, 1963, pp. 137–142.

Kansas History. "Roadside Business: Frank W. McDonald and the Origins of the 'Indian Village,'" by Keith A. Sculle, vol. 14, no. 1, Spring 1991, pp. 15–24 and cover.

Lehigh Valley Motor Club News (AAA), Allentown, Pennsylvania. "And Now! The Cabin Camp," by A. E. Holden, June 1928, pp. 12–13, 46, and 48.

The Literary Digest. "'Tin Can Tourists' Terrifying California," May 16, 1925, pp. 73–76.

Lodging. "Motels," by Dennis E. Bale, June 1985, pp. 90–91, 124–125, and 127.
——. "Kemmons Wilson and the Founding of the Holiday Inn," by David Halberstam, July–August 1993, pp. 30–35 and cover.

Los Angeles Times. "For Tourist Camps, Municipal Grounds Open to Public in Elysian Park," July 3, 1920, part 2, p.1.
——. "City's Auto Tourist Camp Yields Profit," January 2, 1924, part 1, p. 10.
——. "Hostelry Chain for Motorists: 'Motels' Is Name for New Caravansary System," January 18, 1925.
——. "New System Aids Tourists: Roadside 'Motel' Caters to Motorists," February 7, 1926, p. 6.
——. "STANDARDIZED: Motels Going Full Circle–Hotels Again," by Susan J. Diamond, August 28, 1979.

Memphis Press Scimitar. "Tourist Court Began as Sideline in 1929 Expands into Chain Thru the Southwest: Memphis Link Is Newest 'Alamo Plaza,'" by Clark Porteous, August 25, 1939.

Metropolitan Home. "Motel," by Jon Bowermaster, February 1988, p. 41.

Minneapolis Sunday Tribune Picture Magazine. "All Aboard for Nowhere: Sioux Falls, S.D. Has a Novel Motel–It's a Train with Three Sleeping Cars," December 29, 1963, pp. 12–13.

Motor. "Putting Your Home on Wheels," by Harry A. Tarantous, May 1916, pp. 76–77 and 138.

Motor Age. "Three Months' Roughing It in a Motor Car," by Frederick W. Herendeen, September 25, 1913, pp. 20–21.
——. "Camping Out with Your Motor Car," by Frank H. Trego, May 18, 1916, pp. 34–40.

National Petroleum News. "Tourist Camps Pay Southern Jobbers As Rented Dealer Outlets," by Ward K. Halbert, March 20, 1929, pp. 161, 164, 168–169, and 171.
——. "'Gas' Stations Grow to Motorists Hotels Under Pierce Terminal System," by Carleton Whiting, March 19, 1930, pp. 153, 155, 157, and 160–161.

——. "Tourist Camp Stations Patterned After Dutch Windmills," by E. L. Barringer, April 30, 1930, pp. 105–106.
——. "Indian Village to Grow Around Station," by Louis Weller, June 25, 1930, pp. 89 and ff.
——. "Cleanliness, Quiet, Attractiveness–Desired in Tourist Camp," August 12, 1931, pp. 60–63.
——. "Highway Cabin Camps: Article 1," by E. L. Barringer, October 9, 1935, pp. 32–34; "Highway Cabin Camps: Article 2," October 23, 1935, pp. 43–44 and 49; "Danish Village Is Outstanding Highway Camp" (sidebar to Article 2), pp. 49–50; and "Highway Cabin Camps: Article 3," December 25, 1935, pp. 42–43.
——. "Uncle Sam Takes Census of Tourist Camps," by E. L. Barringer, December 15, 1937, pp. 44 and ff.

New York Times. "Hospitality and the Plastic Esthetic," by Ada Louise Huxtable, October 14, 1973.
——. "The First Haven for Man and His Auto" (Milestone Motel), by Joseph Giovannini, July 9, 1987.

Oxford (Mich.) Leader. "The Madonna Inn, San Luis Obispo, Calif.," by Patricia Burton, October 17, 1962, p. 6.

Pacific Coast Travel. "Hotel for Motorists: A Novel and Extremely Practical Idea for Motor Hotels Located a Day's Journey Apart Along the Pacific Highway," by Charles L. Estey, October 1925, p. 29.

Popular Mechanics. "Auto-Bungalow Touring Within Reach of All," by Wm. H. Hunt, March 1921, pp. 136–139 and cover.

Postcard Collector. "Food for Thought" (South of the Border Motel complex), by Jennifer Henderson, September 1994, pp. 32–34.
——. "South of the Border, SC," by Tom Range, December 1994, pp. 16–17.

The Press Dispatch (Kansas City, Mo.). Three-part article by Jack Miles: "Machine Gun Blazing Fight with Bonnie, Clyde in Platte's Past," July 13, 1994, p. 3; "Platte Shoot-out Marked Beginning of End for Bonnie & Clyde" and "Platte Missing Barrow Gang Record," July 20, 1994, p. 3; and "Northland Shoot-out Site Unmarked," July 27, 1994, p. 3.

Progressive Architecture. "Roadside Mecca: Madonna Inn, San Luis Obispo, Calif.," text and photographs by TELETHON, November 1973, pp. 124–129.

San Diego Tribune. "TraveLodge cofounder Scott King Dies at 71," February 19, 1975.

San Francisco Examiner. "Fitting Makes Motor Car Just Like a Pullman" (automobile telescope apartment), February 13, 1916, p. 1A.

San Luis Obispo (Calif.) Daily Telegram. "Motel Opens for Service to Motor Public," December 12, 1925.

Saturday Evening Post. "Adventures in Auto-mobumming," by Sinclair Lewis (three-part article), December 20 and 27, 1919, and January 3, 1920.
——. "Kemmons Wilson: The Inn-Side Story," by Frederic A. Birmingham, Winter 1971.

SCA News. "Wigwams Need New Chief," vol. 1, no. 1, Spring 1993, p. 4.
——. "Coral Court Closes" (noted from *St. Louis Post Dispatch,* August 18 and 22, 1993), vol. 1 no. 4, Winter 1993–94, p. 1.
——. "Letter to the Editor" (Coral Court), by Burr Oxley, vol. 2, no. 3, Fall 1994, p. 5.

SCA News Journal. "Coral Court: A Gem of the Road," vol. 1, nos. 1–3, Fall 1987, pp. 1 and 3.
——. "Tourist Courts" issue, vol. 12, no. 2, Fall 1992. "Accommodating the Traveler: The Development of the Tourist Court on U.S. Route 20 in New York State," by Tania Werbizky, pp. 2–9 and cover; "Camp Grande: The Beginnings of Private Tourist Camps?," by Dwayne Jones, pp. 19–20; "Sources & Resources: *Tourist Court Journal,*" reported by Dwayne Jones, pp. 21–22; and "How Many Tourists Camps and Courts Were There?" compiled by Tania Werbizky, p. 22.

Smithsonian. "America's Home Away from Home Is Still a Good Motel," by Phil Patton, March 1986, pp. 127–136.

Studies in Sociology. Published by The Department of Sociology, Southern Methodist University, Dallas, Texas. "The Urban Tourist Camp," by Elbert L. Hooker, vol. 1, no. 1, Summer 1936, pp. 12–18.

Time. "Rapid Rise of the Host with the Most" (Kemmons Wilson), June 12, 1972, pp. 77–79, 81–82, and cover.

Touring Topics (Automobile Club of Southern California). Delavan Camp House Boon to Motor Travelers," November 1915, p. 20.

Tourist Court Journal. "The Tourist Court of the Future," by Jacob W. Forbes, Montana State Board of Health, December 1939, pp. 8 and ff.
——. "My Most Successful Promotional Ideas," by Paul Young, Wigwam Village No. 7, San Bernardino, Calif., January 1959, p. 49.
——. "Your Pool–Magnet or Mistake?," by Gene Maxwell, March 1959, pp. 75–78.
——. "Cashing In on the Difference" (International Motel, Rochester, Minnesota), April 1959, pp. 65–66, 68, and 70.
——. "Alamo Plaza Motel Chain Grows from 22 to 34 Locations" (advertisement), February 1960, p. 59.

——. "How Off-Beat Theme Sells Rooms & Food" (South of the Border Motel), September 1951, pp. 23–26, 28, and cover.

Trails-a-way. "Cross-country Camping in 1923," by T. L. (Roy) Engle, January, 1986, pp. 3–5 and 8.

Transmission. (Northern Natural Gas Company, Omaha, Nebraska). "Sioux Chief Traintel," vol. 12, no. 2, 1964, pp. 10–11.

Vermilion (Ohio) Photojournal. "Famous Cask Villa Vats," by George Wakefield, October 30, 1989.

Wayside Salesman: A Magazine Devoted to Roadside Merchandising. "Tourist Camps Prove Popular," vol. 1, no. 10, March 1931, pp. 27 and 42 and advertisements on pp. 4, 29, and 41.

Westways (Automobile Club of Southern California). "America's First Tourist Court," by Marvin B. Irwin, June 1954, pp. 10–11.

Wheels, Journal of the National Automotive History Collection, Detroit Public Library, Detroit, Michigan. "Innovators: The Rodome and the Road Home," by James Wren, December 1993, p. 2.

Woman's Home Companion. "Home Away from Home: Vacation Motor Camping in Comfort," by F. E. Brimmer, May 1923, pp. 47–48 and 64.

First Edition   Second Printing, 1996

Some of the illustrations in this book are published with the permission of private collectors, institutions, and corporations who are listed with the source credits beginning on page 123.

Excerpts from "The Great American Roadside" by James Agee (unsigned), *Fortune,* September 1934, reprinted with permission from *Fortune* and the James Agee Trust.

Excerpts from *Travels with Charley* by John Steinbeck, reprinted with the permission of William Heinemann Ltd. and Penguin USA, copyright © 1961, 1962 by The Curtis Publishing Co., © 1962 by John Steinbeck, renewed © 1990 by Elaine Steinbeck, Thom Steinbeck, and John Steinbeck IV, Viking Penguin, a division of Penguin Books USA Inc.

Excerpt from "Hospitality and the Plastic Esthetic," by Ada Louise Huxtable, October 14, 1973, reprinted with the permission of Ada Louise Huxtable, and copyright © by The New York Times Company. Reprinted by permission.

ISBN 0-8212-2162-0
Library of Congress Catalog Card Number 95-77074

Bulfinch Press is an imprint and trademark of Little, Brown and Company (Inc.)

Published simultaneously in Canada by Little, Brown & Company (Canada) Limited

Design by Eric Baker Design Associates, Inc.

Printed in Singapore